THE FIRESIDE

A Historical and Spiritual Drama in One Act

By

Eileen DiStasio-Clark

Permissions

Correlation Intellectual Property

The Church of Jesus Christ of Latter-day Saints

50 E. North Temple Street

Salt Lake City, UT 84150-0005

Phone: 801-240-3959

Fax: 801-240-1187

DEDICATION

With Great Love and Appreciation To and For…

My Family:

My Parents (now deceased),

Joseph DeStasio Sr. & Miriam Lucille Baragone DeStasio Andrea Jean DeStasio.

My older sister, McIntosh.

My younger and only brother, Joseph DeStasio Jr.

My younger sister, Donna Marie DeStasio Wagner

My Children:

Eileen, Rebekah, Rachel, S. Michael,

Jennifer, Sharon, Tara, Stephanie,

Apryll, Mikaelah, & M. Trevor

and THEIR Families!!

And to All Those…

The Casts and Crews,

who took part in the three original performances

1986/1996/2004

ABOUT THE AUTHOR

Eileen DiStasio-Clark is the second oldest of four children. She is the mother of eleven children and grandmother to twenty-four grandchildren, to date. As a member of The Church of Jesus Christ of Latter-Day Saints, she serves in various positions, teaching, leading, and ministering to children, youth, and adults. Currently, she is also a Family History Missionary. Eileen established the Pursuit of Excellence Institute of Family Education, a non-profit organization focused on strengthening the family. Presently she holds an A.A., a B.A., and an M.A. in Clinical Psychology and is working on the completion of her Doctoral Degree.

FOREWORD

Early in the summer of 1986, the Ward Mission Leader in the Jacksonville Ward of The Church of Jesus Christ of Latter-Day Saints, in Jacksonville, Florida, where my family lived at that time, formulated the idea of presenting a play which would inspire church members and whomever else participated in its presentation, either as part of the cast and crew or as a member of the audience. He asked me to write a play based on the stories in the Book of Mormon. He knew he wanted the story of the Savior's visit to the Americas to appear as the final scene, but as to the choice of the rest of the contents, he left that to me.

I would have plenty of time to do this, I had told myself because it was not going to be presented until September. However, with a busy home, schooling my children, and other church responsibilities to fill my time, the summer slipped away rather quickly. When the calendar showed that I had only three weeks left before the scheduled performance, I became concerned that I would not be able to search through the Book of Mormon for the right stories to use, select a cast, and hold enough rehearsals to produce a good play. With this on my mind and a prayer in my heart, I sat down at my computer on a Friday evening around 9:00 p.m., and by 5:00 a.m. Saturday morning, the body of the play was completed. And, miraculously, the performance was amazing!

Additional character notes, the list of properties, a few additional stories, and detailed instructions were formulated and added to the script during our first two productions of the play. Thereafter, the perfecting polish was completed and displayed in the following two productions of THE FIRESIDE.

It is my testimony to you that it was through the guidance of the Lord's Spirit that THE FIRESIDE was written. It is my hope that through that same Spirit, this play will be performed often and everywhere, aiding many in their efforts to live their own lives better and to more successfully share the great gift of the Gospel of Jesus the Christ with others.

It is to be noted that in any performance, THE FIRESIDE is to be enacted as it is written with no alterations.

THE FIRESIDE
A Historical and Spiritual Drama in One Act
For Nineteen Speaking and Sixty-nine Non-Speaking Men,

Ten Speaking and Twelve Non-Speaking Women

Fourteen Non-Speaking Children

Many Extras

A Children's Chorus and A Choir

CAST MEMBERS

Speaking

Daniel Taylor……………………………………………………………………… the Fireside Speaker

Tracy Taylor………………………………………………………...…...…… Daniel's wife

Heather Taylor………………………………………………….……the Taylor's oldest daughter

Laurel Taylor…………………………………...………………………the Taylor's second daughter

Holly Taylor……………………………………………………the Taylor's youngest daughter

Wayne Stewart………………………………………………………….. the Fireside Host

Shannon Stewart……………………………………………………...……………Wayne's wife

Kellie Haydon………………………………………………………..the Stewart's housekeeper

Autumn McKay…………………………………………………………...…..a friend of Heather

Ryan Perry…………………………...……………………………….a friend of Autumn's family

Amber Perry……………………………………………………………………...…Ryan's wife

Lehi……………………………………………………………………a Hebrew prophet

Sariah………………………………………………………………………...…...Lehi's wife

Laman…………………………………………………………………….....their eldest son

Lemuel………………………………………………………...…………..their second son

King Benjamin……………………………………………………..a Nephite prophet-king

Mary (sings a Capella) …………………………………………………………the mother of Jesus

Abinadi……………………………………………………………….……..a Nephite prophet

King Noah…………………………………………………………...a wicked Nephite king

First Priest…………………………………………………………………...a wicked priest of Noah

Second Priest………………………………...……..………………………a wicked priest of Noah

Ammon…………………………………………………………………one of the sons of Mosiah

First Servant………………………………………..…………………a servant of King Lamoni

Second Servant…………………………………………………………a servant of King Lamoni

King Lamoni………………………………………………...…………a Lamanite King

Samuel the Lamanite……………………………………………..………………a Lamanite prophet

Moroni………………………………………………………..………the last Nephite leader

4

Jared………………………………………………………..………the leader of the Jaredites

Brother of Jared……………………………………………………the first Jaredite prophet

Non-Speaking

Five Prophets………………………………..……………………………prophets of Jerusalem

Sam…………………………………………,……………………………..Nephi's older brother

Nephi……………………………………...Son of Lehi, the great prophet and leader of the Nephites

Laban…………………………………………………………custodian of the Brass Plates

Zoram…………………………………………………………….....a servant of Laban

Three Guards…………………………………………………………...……of Laban

Joseph……………………………………………………………..Husband of Mary

Three Hebrew Men……………………………………………..to be healed by Jesus

Eight Hebrew Women…………………………………………to be healed by Jesus

Six Hebrew Children…………………………………………….to be healed by Jesus

Nine Priests…………………………………………………………....of Noah

Two Guards…………………………………………………………...of Noah

Alma…………………………………….a priest of Noah, Nephite prophet, founder of the church

Alma the Younger……………………………………………………………..son of Alma

Four Sons of Mosiah…………………..……………………………….....friends of Alma the Younger

Four Guards……………………………………………………………..of Lamoni

Ten Servants…………………………………………………….representing Lamanite servants

Heleman…………………………………………………………….a military commander

Twenty Soldiers……………………………………………...representing Stripling Warriors

Two Men…………………………………………..………………….friends of Jared

Four Women……………………………………………wives of Jared, his brother, and their friends

Eight Children……………………………………………………………………….Jaredites

Recorded Voices

Voice of an Angel……………………..…...speaking to Alma the Younger and the Sons of Mosiah

Voice of God…………………………………………………………...Heavenly Father

Voice of Jesus……………………………………..………..as Old Testament God and as the Savior

Extras

Twenty Additional Men (suggested number)..........................Multitudes of Ancient America

Thirty Additional Women (suggested number).......................Multitudes of Ancient America

Fifteen Additional Children (suggested number)....................Multitudes of Ancient America

Two Pre-Selected Audience Members...to offer Prayer

Choruses

Twelve Primary Children (minimum)...............Children's Chorus to sing BOM scene preludes

Twelve Youth/Adults (minimum)..........................Chorus to sing production prelude music

SETTING

Place: The living room of the Stewart home

The 'living stories' take place in Ancient Jerusalem and Ancient America

Time: The present

The 'living stories' take place between 600 B.C. and 33 A.D.

SYNOPSIS

Scene One:	The living room of the Stewart home. Early in the evening. Guests arrive. The fireside begins.	
Scene Two:	**OBTAINING THE BRASS PLATES OF LABAN**	
Sub-scene One:	A camp in the wilderness. Evening hours. About 600 B.C. Lehi sends his sons back to Jerusalem.	
Sub-scene Two:	Laban's house in ancient Jerusalem. Evening hours. About 600 B.C. Laban refuses to give the Brass Plates to Laman. Nephi and his brothers return to their homes for their gold, silver, and precious things with which to buy the plates. Laban still refuses, but sends his guards to kill them and steal their riches. They escape. Nephi returns, kills Laban, gets the plates, and returns to his brothers with Zoram.	
Sub-scene Three:	A camp in the wilderness. Late evening hours. About 600 B.C. Nephi and his brothers return to their father.	
Scene Three:	The living room of the Stewart home. Early in the evening. The fireside continues.	
Scene Four:	**KING BENJAMIN SPEAKS TO HIS PEOPLE**	
Sub-scene One:	Ancient America, outside the temple in the land of Zarahemla. Daytime. Around 124 B.C. King Benjamin is speaking to his people.	
Sub-scene Two:	A stable in Bethlehem. In the night. The Nativity.	
Sub-scene Three:	A street in Jerusalem. Daytime. Around 33 A.D. Jesus in ministering among the people	
Sub-scene Four:	The Garden of Gethsemane. In the night. Around 33 A.D.	
Sub-scene Five:	Ancient America, outside the temple in the Land of Zarahemla. Daytime. Around 124 B.C. King Benjamin continues to speak to his people.	
Scene Five:	The living room of the Stewart home.	

A little later in the evening. The fireside continues.

Scene Six:	**ABINADI WARNS THE PEOPLE**
	Ancient America. The Land of Nephi. Around 148 B.C.
Scene Seven:	**ABINADI WARNS KING NOAH**
	Ancient America. The court of King Noah, in the Land of Nephi.
	Around 148 B.C.
Scene Eight:	**ALMA BAPTIZES**
	Ancient America. The Waters of Mormon. Around 147 B.C.
Scene Nine:	The living room of the Stewart home. A little later in the evening
	The fireside continues.
Scene Ten:	**THE CONVERSION OF ALMA THE YOUNGER AND THE FOUR SONS OF MOSIAH**
Sub-scene One:	Ancient America. The Land of Zarahemla.
	Probably between 100 and 92 B.C.
	An angel visits Alma the Younger and the four sons of Mosiah.
Sub-scene Two:	Ancient America. The Land of Zarahemla. The chambers of
	Alma the Elder. Probably between 100 and 92 B.C.
	Alma learns of his son's experience.
Scene Eleven:	The living room of the Steward home. Later in the evening.
	The fireside continues.
Scene Twelve:	**AMMON'S MISSION TO THE LAMANITE COUNTRY**
	Ancient America. The Land of Ishmael. King Lamoni's throne room.
	About 90 B.C. Ammon is brought before King Lamoni.
	He desires to serve the Lamanite King.
Scene Thirteen:	**AMMON AT THE WATERING PLACE**
	Ancient America. The Land of Ishmael. King About 90 B.C.
	Ammon protects the king's flocks from the wicked herdsman.
Scene Fourteen:	**AMMON TEACHES KING LAMONI**
	Ancient America. The Land of Ishmael. King Lamoni's throne room.
	Ammon teaches the Lamanites.
Scene Fifteen:	The living room of the Stewart home. Later in the evening

The fireside continues.

Scene Sixteen:	**HELAMAN AND THE STRIPLING WARRIORS**
	Ancient America. The Land of Zarahemla. Around 62 B.C.
	Helaman organizes an army of Lamanite Youth.
Scene Seventeen:	The living room of the Stewart home. Later in the evening.
	The fireside continues.
Scene Eighteen:	**SAMUEL THE LAMANITE WARNS THE NEPHITES**
	The city wall of Zarahemla. Around 6 B.C.
Scene Nineteen:	The living room of the Stewart home. Late in the evening.
	The fireside continues.
Scene Twenty:	**THE STORY OF THE JAREDITES**

	Sub-scene One:	Ancient America. In the wilderness. Between 400 and 421 A.D.
		Moroni is abridging the Plates of Ether.
	Sub-scene Two:	The Land of Shinar.
		Around the time of the destruction of the Tower of Babel.
		The Jaredites are led to the Promised Land.

Scene Twenty-one:	The living room of the Stewart home. Late in the evening.
	The fireside continues.
Scene Twenty-two:	**THE COMING OF CHRIST TO THE AMERICAS**
	The City of Zarahemla. The site of the temple ruins. Around 33 A.D.
	The Savior visits Ancient America.
Scene Twenty-three:	The living room of the Stewart home. Late in the evening.
	The fireside ends with prayer.

Note: All 'living stories' scenes, which take place in Ancient America or Ancient Jerusalem, occur within the 'mists of a vision' created by dry ice.

NOTES ON CHARACTERS AND COSTUMES

Daniel: He is an attractive, self-conscious man, soft-spoken, with an air of spirituality about him. He is a perfectionist. He is in his mid to late forties. He wears a dark, three-piece suit and tie. In Scene Nine, he removes his jacket

Tracy: She is a dependable, supportive wife, also in her mid to late forties. She presents the appearance of a spiritual woman who is very successful at everything she attempts. Her dress is modestly styled and brightly colored; one she might wear for church.

Heather: Intelligent and well-mannered, Heather is a mature young woman of about 20. She is both liked and respected by her peers. She appreciates beautiful, obviously feminine clothing and expresses this in the appropriately adorned, pastel, mid-length ensemble she wears.

Laurel: Laurel is in her later teens, vivacious and friendly, blessed with the ability to see humor in everything. She enjoys life to the fullest while staying close to divine principles. Casual but well dressed, she wears nice-looking pants or shorts (knee-length or capri) ensemble in warm colors. Opting to sit on the floor, she removes her shoes almost as soon as she is seated.

Holly: Holly is a quiet, playful, and helpful young teen or pre-teen. It is obvious from the closeness she keeps to Daniel that she is "Daddy's Little Girl." She likes her clothing simple but bold, as is seen in the very brightly colored T-shirt and pants or shorts (knee-length or capri) she wears.

Wayne: Short and happy, Wayne is an outgoing, delightful person with an enviable sense of humor. Having previously been frustrated by the many trials of life, now in his mid-sixties, he is like a child with a new toy since discovering the gospel of Jesus the Christ. He is uneasy sharing personal experiences, but generous with his love. He wears very comfortable sports clothes and slippers.

Shannon: She is in her fifties, a little on the quiet side, but very generous and thoughtful. She keeps her home in order, but does not allow it to look or feel like a museum. She wears a comfortable, full-length, softly colored, house dress and slippers.

Kellie:	Her age is indeterminate, making it possible for a woman of almost any age to portray her. She is single, soft-spoken and very down-to-earth. She wears jeans and a coolly colored oversized blouse.
Autumn:	A college graduate in her early to mid-twenties, she is very self-assured and possesses a positive outlook on life. Though she is neither overbearing nor offensive, she displays a professional demeanor. She wears a modest, professionally-styled skirt in a quiet floral pattern and pull-over vest with a color-coordinated blouse.
Ryan:	He is a very sober, highly educated professional man in his early thirties. He misses all humor that is not pointed out to him, but possesses a deep concern for living right. He wears a handsome two-piece sports suit in medium colors.
Amber:	She is an even-tempered, moderately out-spoken woman in her late twenties with a ravenous appetite for knowledge. She is the perfect counter-part for Ryan, as she views all things in life through the eyes of a humorist. She wears an 'at-home' ensemble in eye-catching pastel colors.
Lehi:	A very strong man, both physically and spiritually, he possesses the vigor of a man, perhaps between forty and fifty years old, but the appearance of a man in hislater years. He has a long white beard and mustache. He wears a long-sleeved, full-length, red tunic, the bodice of which is adorned with a gold braid, a black waistband, and a red veil bound with a gold and black headband. (Colors may vary according to available materials, however, the appearance of comfortable affluence as would have been exhibited in ancient days must be maintained.)
Sariah:	She is a sturdy woman with the appearance of maturity. She wears a long-sleeved, full-length, olive-green tunic, which is adorned with silver 'lace' around the neckline, sleeve cuffs, and hemline. Her veil is white. (Colors may vary according to available materials, however the appearance of comfortable affluence as would have been exhibited in ancient days must be maintained.)
Laman:	He possesses great physical strength and an air of wickedness. His appearance is that of a man in his thirties, one who enjoys the 'blessings' of the world. He wears a mid-shin length tunic in a dull green or orange shade. The hem is trimmed with ivory tassels, and around the waist is wrapped in a broad black leather band. The

veil is ivory or off-white with a black leather headband. Wide gold bracelets are worn just above the wrists. (Colors may vary according to available materials, however, the appearance of comfortable affluence as would have been exhibited in ancient days must be maintained. Additionally, the accuracy of color is not as important as the appearance of temporal mindedness.)

Lemuel: He possesses great physical strength and an air of wickedness. His appearance is that of a man in his thirties, one who enjoys the 'blessings' of the world. He wears a mid-shin length tunic in a dull green or orange shade. The hem is trimmed with ivory tassels and around the waist and is wrapped in a broad black leather band. The veil is ivory or off-white with a black leather headband. Wide gold bracelets are worn just above the wrists. (Colors may vary according to available materials, however, the appearance of comfortable affluence as would have been exhibited in ancient days must be maintained. Additionally, the accuracy of color is not as important as the appearance of temporal mindedness.)

Note: Laman and Lemuel should not wear exactly the same costumes.

King Benjamin: He is a tall, slender man with the appearance of a man in his mid-fifties. He has a long black beard and mustache. He wears a long pale blue tunic with a white waistband and a cardigan-style, full-length red robe. His red headband is adorned with a large gold plume.

Mary: A small and gentle woman in her late teens or early twenties. She has long dark hair and wears a full-length white tunic with a full-length bright blue veil.

Abinadi: A man of small stature but a powerful demeanor. He may be between fifty and sixty and has a white beard and mustache. He wears a mid-shin length, brown skirt bound at the waist with an orange band and an ivory tunic-style shirt. His robe is medium blue. The robe must be able to be removed and wrist-to-ankle chains must be able to be put on quickly between scenes.

King Noah: He is a heavy, full-bearded man in his forties or fifties. His appearance is dark, wicked, and oppressive. He wears a mid-length, deep purple tunic with gold tassel trim, bound at the waist with a broad, jeweled silver belt. His cape is scarlet with gold shoulder clasps. Gold braid trims the sleeve

	cuffs. His crown, which fans open on the sides, is gold, heavily jeweled, and topped with gold, white, and green plumes. He wears rings and wristbands of jeweled gold.
Priests:	Their ages may vary. They wear long black tunics bound at the waist with gold bands and adorned with gold yokes. Their hats are tall and black with green, gold, and red bands, and gold neck drapes. They also wear gold wristbands and rings.
Ammon:	He is a strong, powerful looking man, probably in his thirties. In scene ten, he wears a very richly adorned, full-length, long-sleeved, bright turquoise tunic. The sleeve cuffs and hemline are trimmed with gold braid, and the waist is bound with a long gold cord. He wears rings and chains of gold. In scene twelve, he wears a knee-length, ivory tunic with brown tassels around the hem, and bound at the waist with a very broad leather band. He wears a leather sheath which crosses his chest and a leather headband.
Lamoni's Servants:	Their ages may vary. They are strong and dark. They wear knee-length leather skirts and ivory tunic-style shirts.
King Lamoni:	He is a thin but lean man, perhaps in his fifties or sixties. He wears a full-length, mid-length-sleeved, red or dark orange tunic, with bright yellow tasseled trim around the sleeve cuffs and the hemline. His headdress is made of colorful feathers and fits like a boy's winter muffler cap.
Samuel the Lamanite:	He is of indeterminate age, strong and commanding in appearance. He wears a brown knee-length tunic, a brass chest plate, and a red cape. He also wears brass wristbands and carries a staff.
Moroni:	He is a man of large stature and great spiritual strength. He is perhaps in his thirties or forties. He wears a pale-yellow full-length skirt, trimmed at the hemline with blue tassels, and bound at the waist with a black band. His shirt is a blue tunic-style top with silver or gold studs around the neckline and sleeve cuffs. He wears a pale yellow headband and one very broad metal wristband.
Jared:	He is strong and imposing. He could be in his twenties or thirties. He wears a short, just below the knees, half-tunic of brown or black fur with an olive-green

14

shirt. His waistband is broad and red in color. His hat is short and red with a black and gold band and an ivory neck drape, tasseled on the edges.

Brother of Jared: He is strong and imposing. He could be in his twenties or thirties. He wears a short, just below the knees, half-tunic of brown or black fur with an olive-green shirt. His waistband is broad and red in color. His hat is short and red with a black and gold band and an ivory neck drape, tasseled on the edges.

Hebrew Prophets: They are older men, spiritual and courageous. They wear full-length, long-sleeved white tunics, bound at the waist by long black sashes. Their robes are 1) bright red with one black stripe, 2) blue with one black stripe, 3) bright green with one black stripe, 4) bright orange with one black stripe, and 5) bright purple with one black stripe. They each carry a staff.

Sam: He possesses great physical strength and an air of great spirituality. He possesses the appearance of a man in his late twenties. He wears a mid-shin length tunic in bright green or orange with silver braid trim around the sleeve cuffs and hemline. Over the tunic is worn a mid-thigh length leather vest, bound at the waist with a leather band. The vest laces on the front bodice. A narrow headband of dark braid is worn without a veil. Brass studded, broad leather bracelets are won just above the wrists.

Nephi: He is a man of large stature and great spiritual strength. He possesses the appearance of a man in his late twenties. He wears a mid-shin length tunic in bright green or orange with silver braid trim around the sleeve cuffs and hemline. Over the tunic is worn a mid-thigh length leather vest, bound at the waist with a leather band. The vest laces on the front bodice. A narrow headband of dark braid is worn without a veil. Brass studded, broad leather bracelets are worn just above the wrists.

Note: Sam and Nephi should not wear exactly the same costumes.

Laban: A dark man of large stature and imposing demeanor, perhaps in his forties. He wears a dark tunic bound at the waist with a bright yellow sash, a black cape, brass armbands and gold chains and rings.

Zoram: He is a man of large stature. His age is indeterminate. He wears a knee-length tan tunic bound at the waist with a bright band. He wears a headband the color of the waist band. He wears heavy metal wristbands.

Laban's Guards: All are men of large stature. Their ages are indeterminate. They wear short tunics, knee-length, in dark colors bound at the waist with black bands. They wear heavy metal wristbands and swords in black sheaths.

Joseph: Strong and quiet, he is a man, perhaps in his mid to late twenties. He wears a full-length dark blue robe over a full-length white tunic, bound at the waist with a light blue sash.

Note: **No** exceptions should be made in the costuming of Joseph.

Hebrews: The men, women, and children being ministered to by the Savior wear full-length, mid-length, or knee-length tunics in a variety of pale colors with brighter, color-coordinated sashes and trim. The women wear white or ivory veils.

King Noah's Guards: They are strong men of indeterminate ages. They wear knee-length purple tunics, bound at the waist, just below metal breastplates, with a broad red band, worn under a more narrow gold studded brown band.
Their helmets are of brass and cover the neck. The top is plumed.

Alma: He is a thin, lean man of average height, perhaps in his fifties.
In scene seven, he wears the attire of the priests, but must be able to remove the black tunic to reveal a full-length white tunic for scene eight. In scene ten he wears a mid-shin length deep blue tunic bound at the waist with a narrow gold band. His turban-style headdress is white and has a neck drape.

Alma the Younger: He is a strong, powerful looking man, probably in his thirties. He wears a very richly adorned, full-length, long-sleeved, vivid peach tunic. The sleeve cuffs and hemline are trimmed with gold braid, and the waist is bound with a long gold cord. He wears rings and chains of gold.

Sons of Mosiah: They are strong, powerful men, probably in their thirties. They wear very richly adorned, full-length, long-sleeved, bright blue, orange, and yellow tunics. The sleeve cuffs and hemlines are trimmed with gold braid, and the waists are bound with long gold cords. They wear rings and chains of gold.

King Lamoni's Guards: They are strong, fearless-looking men. They wear knee-length, brown tunics, bound at the waist with gold and black bands. They carry spears and knives.

Helaman: He is a very strong and powerful-looking man, with the appearance of righteousness. He wears a short beard and moustache. He wears a green, knee-length skirt and ivory tunic-style shirt, trimmed at the sleeve cuffs with gold bands. A metal breastplate covers his chest and is bound at the waist by a feather-edged brown belt and red sash. Heavy metal wristbands are worn along with a metal helmet bound with a red plume and a red cape. He carries a shield and a sword. (If possible, he rides a horse.)

Warriors: Their ages may vary; however, they are all young and strong. They wear tan, tunic-style shirts and knee-length striped skirts in various colors, bound at the waist by broad sashes and trimmed with tassels. They wear heavy metal wristbands and gold headbands and carry sheathed knives, spears, and shields.

Jaredites: They wear full-length, mid-length, or knee-length tunics of ivory or brown, bound at the waist with cords of various colors. The tunics are trimmed with bands and cords in a variety of colors and combinations, but all are simple. Some of the Jaredites may also wear robes of blues and browns, and the women wear long veils.

Multitudes: They wear full-length tunics of white, ivory, or pastels, bound at the waist with coordinating sashes and robes in colors to match the sashes. The women may wear veils.

Children's Chorus: They wear mid-shin length, deep green tunics bound at the waist with bright gold sashes and trimmed at the hemline and sleeve cuffs with gold. They also wear headbands of green and gold.

Youth and Adult Chorus: They wear full-length white tunics bound at the waist with maroon sashes. Their robes are maroon.

Jesus: As a baby, the infant should be wrapped in a soft white blanket. As a man: He wears a full-length, white tunic, bound at the waist with a brown cord, and a scarlet robe.

As a resurrected being, He wears a full-length, bright, shiny white tunic with a bright, shiny white robe.

Note: All footwear for the 'living stories' characters should be either sandals or moccasins. Simple jewelry and other accessories can also be added in moderation. It is always important to remember the period and not add anything which would not have been worn in that time. Though there were periods of great wealth, modest simplicity should be portrayed overall. Only certain scenes and characters should appear in riches, and that, for a contrasting effect of the spiritual and temporal.

The costuming, as described above, was chosen as a result of a study of inspired Book of Mormon pictures, and such could and should be consulted before costumes are sewn. An attempt was made to use color to the advantage of the production, making the overall effect a more appealing one, without straying from period accuracy. It is not so important what colors you choose as it is that the blend of colors in each scene enhances rather than detracts from the action and message of that scene and does not appear contemporary.

STAGE POSITIONS

UPSTAGE means away from the footlights or toward the back of the stage.

DOWNSTAGE means toward the footlights or front of the stage.

STAGE-RIGHT is used to reference the actor as he or she faces the audience.

STAGE-LEFT is used to reference the actor as he or she faces the audience.

> **U** means Upstage.
>
> **UR** means Upstage-Right
>
> **URC** means Upstage-Right-Center
>
> **UC** means Upstage-Center
>
> **UCL** means Upstage-Center-Left
>
> **UL** means Upstage-Left
>
> **R** means Stage-Right.
>
> **RC** means Centerstage-Right
>
> **C** means Centerstage
>
> **LC** means Centerstage-Left
>
> **L** means Stage-Left
>
> **D** means Downstage
>
> **DR** means Downstage-Right
>
> **DRC** means Downstage-Right-Center
>
> **DC** means Downstage-Center
>
> **DCL** means Downstage-Left-Center
>
> **DL** means Downstage-Left

The 'living stories' are presented on the stage or amidst the audience. Directions for action which takes place among the audience are used with reference to the actor as he faces the stage.

The fireside is enacted on a Platform erected in front of and to the left of the stage. Directions for action which takes place on the platform are used in the same manner as for action which takes place on the stage. When attention is drawn away from or back to the platform, **P** is used to designate **PLATFORM.**

A designated stage position refers to a general area, not a specific point.

19

NOTE: To save time, speed up rehearsals and reduce the amount of directions needed by the actors, be certain everyone functionally understands the meanings and positions indicated by these basic terms and abbreviations. If necessary, chalk or tape off stage positions and walk your actors from position to position until they are familiar with them.

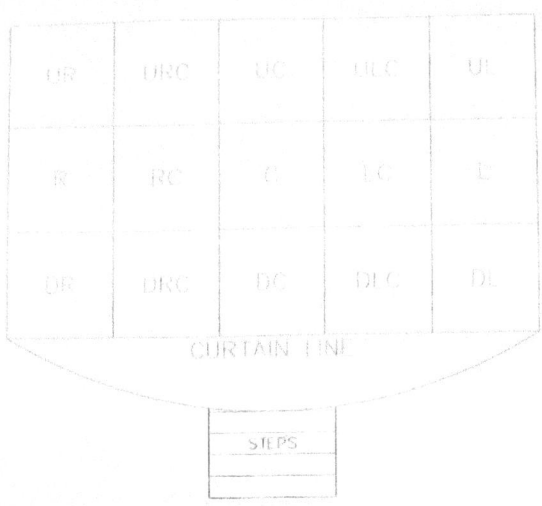

UR	URC	UC	ULC	UL
R	RC	C	LC	L
DR	DRC	DC	DLC	DL

CURTAIN LINE

STEPS

CHART OF STAGE POSITIONS - PLATFORM AND STAGE

UR	URC	UC	ULC	UL
R	RC	C	LC	L
DR	DRC	DC	DLC	DL

PROSCENIUM

CHART OF STAGE POSITIONS - AUDITORIUM

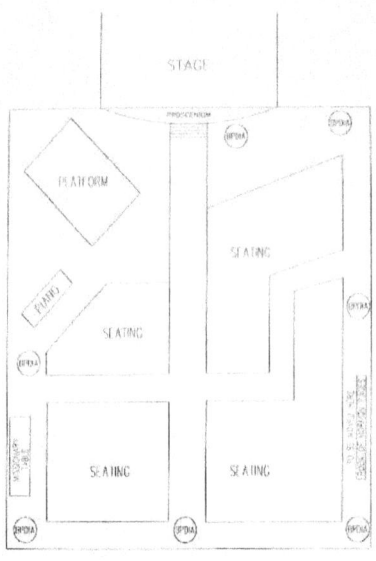

STAGE CHART - AUDITORIUM
AUDIENCE ARRANGEMENT

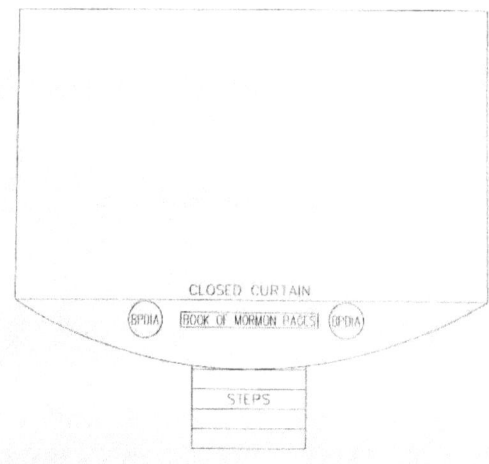

STAGE CHART - PROSCENIUM

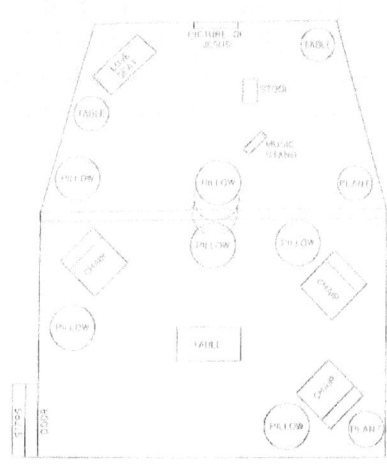

STAGE CHART - PLATFORM
Scenes: 1,3,5,9,11,15,17,19,21 & 23

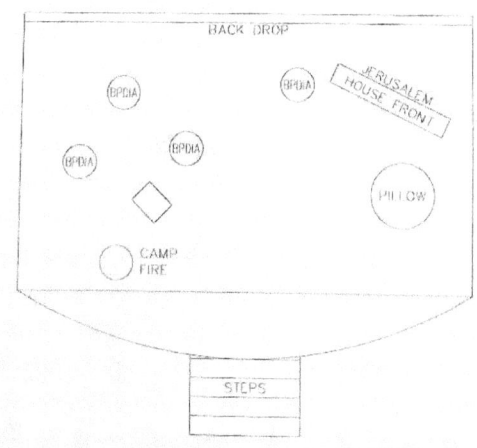

STAGE CHART - SCENE TWO

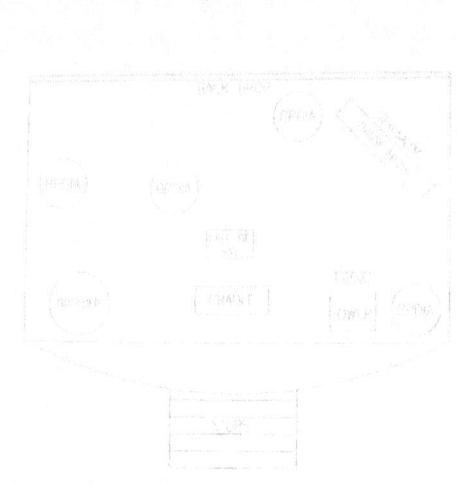

STAGE CHART - SCENE FOUR

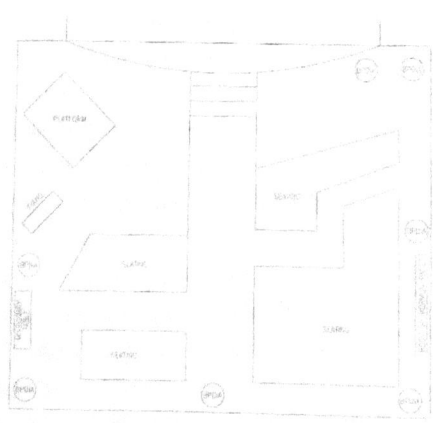

STAGE CHART - SCENE SIX AND THIRTEEN

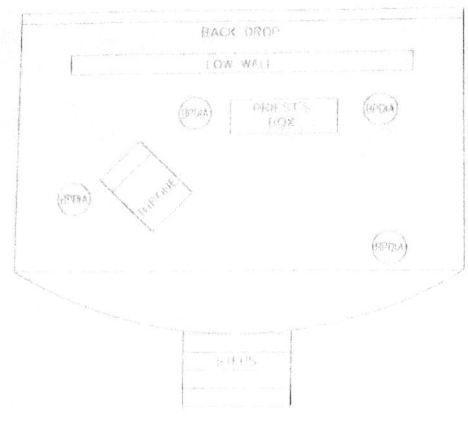

STAGE CHART - SCENE SEVEN

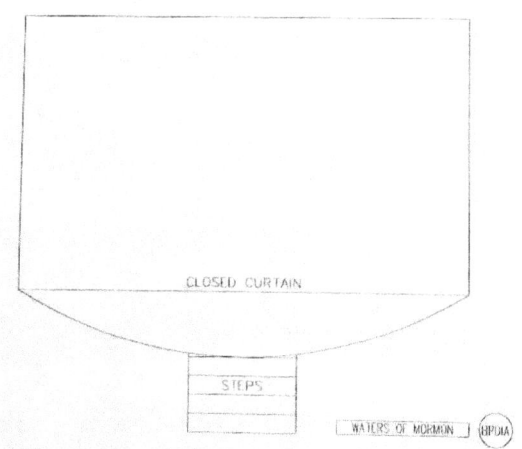

STAGE CHART - SCENE EIGHT

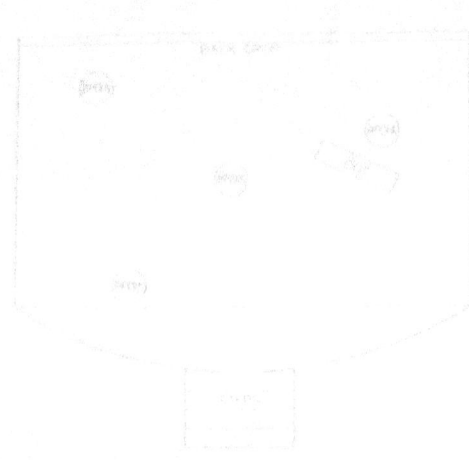

STAGE CHART - SCENE TEN

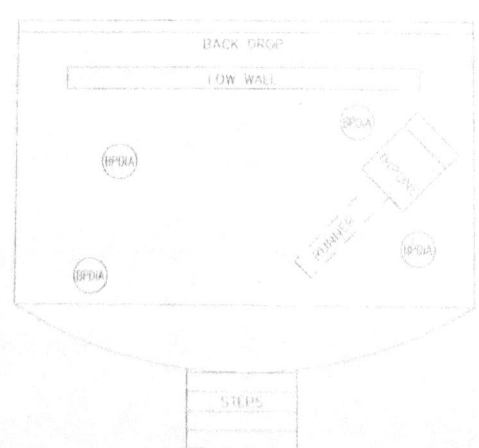

STAGE CHART - SCENE TWELVE AND FOURTEEN

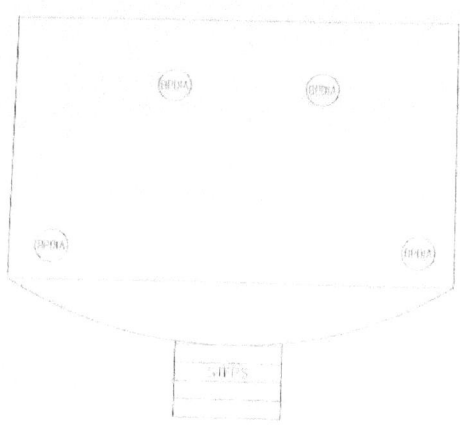

STAGE CHART - SCENE SIXTEEN

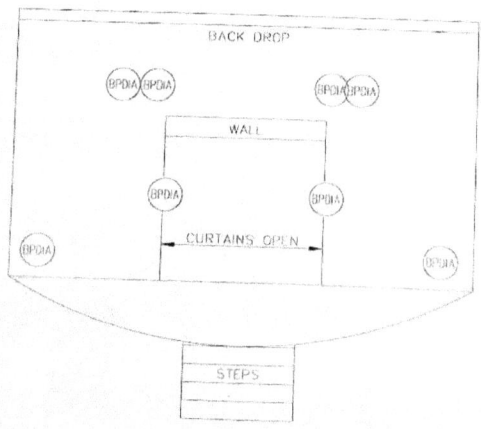

STAGE CHART - SCENE EIGHTEEN

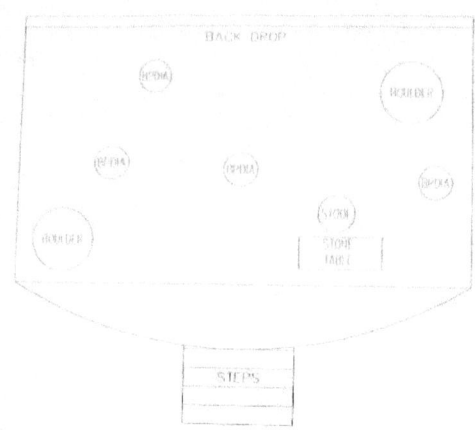

SCENE CHART - SCENE TWENTY

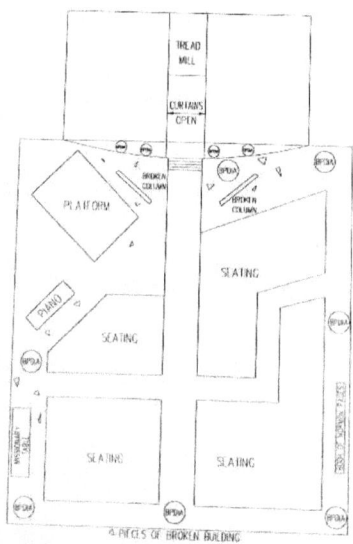

STAGE CHART - SCENE TWENTY-TWO

28

PROPERTIES

All large scenery items and small items not carried on stage by actors, are depicted on the stage charts. The following list of properties are those not part of the scenery, which are placed by the props crew or carried onto the set by the cast.

On Platform: Several Liahona magazines; A Jesus figurine; Small knick-knacks; Several books: A set of Scriptures with a Book of Mormon on the top

For BOM Pages: Two snapshots of each actor, one in Sunday dress, the other in costume;

Scene Two: Several sticks for poking the fire; Two or Three bowls of finger food

Scene Seven: A small round rug; Several goblets; A plumed whip; "Large Cats"

Scenes 12 and 14: A long runner rug, A bowl of grapes, and nuts

Scene Thirteen: Several Sheep

Scene Sixteen: Twenty each of shields, spears, and swords; Thirty-four knives in sheaths

Scene Eighteen: Stones

Scene Twenty: A set of Gold Plates and several loose Gold Plates; An engraving tool; A few scrolls, A candle

Wayne: A pitcher of water, Small paper cups, Napkins

Shannon: A dusting cloth; Sheets of music (the opening song); A plate of refreshments, i.e., mini quiche pies, finger sandwiches, etc.; A needlework project

Daniel: A briefcase from which he removes notes: A pen; A set of Scriptures A Book of Mormon

Tracy: A set of Scriptures, A purse, A plate of cookies or brownies

Heather: Two scrolls, A Liahona, A purse, A set of Scriptures

Laurel: Three sets of Gold Plates, A purse, A set of Scriptures

Holly: One set of Gold Plates, A set of Brass Plates, A set of Scriptures

Kellie: A bowl of snack mix, A set of keys

Autumn: A Portfolio Pad

Ryan: A Book of Mormon

Amber: A purse, A vase of cut flowers

Laman: Three bags of gold, A silver tray, A small box of jewels

Lemuel: Three bags of gold, a pair of silver goblets, a few ropes of jewels

Sam: Five bags of gold, A silver bowl

Nephi: Three bags of gold, Several ropes of jewels, A chest of spices

Laban: A sword with a gold hilt; A goblet

Zoram: A large ring of keys; Brass Plates

Laban's Guards: Swords in sheaths

Hebrews (being healed)**:** A crutch; Wrappings; A cane; A mat; A very thin blanket

Abinadi: Ankle-to-wrist chains and shackles, which he wears

King Noah: A goblet, A bowl of grapes

Noah's Guards: Swords in sheaths; Spears

Ammon: Cords with which his hands are bound; A Sword and Sheath

Lamoni's Guards: Spears; Knives in sheaths

Lamanite Servants: Clubs; Satchels with stones; Slingshots

Helaman: A sword in a sheath; A shield

Samuel the Lamanite: A staff

The Brother of Jared: 16 Smooth White Stones

Children's Chorus: Tom-Toms; Beaded necklaces

MUSIC

To invite the Lord's Spirit, and to set the mood for **THE FIRESIDE**, the following songs have been selected to be sung by a Youth/Adult Choir as Prelude Music.

IN THE HOLLOW OF THY HAND

Monita Turley Robinson and Janice Kapp Perry, Copyright 1977, Prime Recordings

AT THEIR MOHTER'S KNEE

Gail LeBaron Christensen and Janice Kapp Perry, Copyright 1978, Prime Recordings

HOW DOES A SERVANT SHOW HIS LOVE

Janice Kapp, Copyright 1980, Prime Recordings

NO ORDINARY MAN

Janice Kapp Perry, Copyright 1985, Prime Recordings

THE TEST

Janice Kapp Perry V B, Copyright 1985, Prime Recordings

HIS IMAGE IN YOUR COUNTENANCE

Janice Kapp Perry, Copyright 1985, Prime Recordings

LIVE THAT YE MAY ATTAIN

Janice Kapp Perry, Copyright 1985, Prime Recordings

MY WAYS ARE NOT THY WAYS

Jack R. Kapp and Janice Kapp Perry, Copyright 1989, Prime Recordings

JUST WHEN I NEED YOU

Janice Kapp Perry, Copyright 1989, Prime Recordings

DO NOT RUN FASTER

Janice Kapp Perry, Copyright 1989, Prime Recordings

WELL DONE, THOU GOOD AND FAITHFUL SERVANT

Janice Kapp Perry, Copyright 1980, Prime Recordings

MUSIC

Production music includes the following selections:

Scene One: **SEARCH, PONDER, AND PRAY**

#109, LDS Children's Songbook 2014 Edition

Jaclyn Thomas Milne and Carol Baker Black

Copyright 1986 LDS Church

Opening song at the fireside and for the presentation

Sung by the cast and audience

THE LORD IS MY SHEPHERD

#108, LDS Hymn Book 1985 Edition

James Montgomery and Thomas Koschat

Music only; Background for Wayne's testimony

Scene Two: **BOOK OF MORMON STORIES**

#118 LDS Children's Songbook 2014 Edition

Elizabeth F. Bates

Copyright 1969, 1986 LDS Church

First and Second Verses are sung by Children's Chorus: Scene Opener

LORD, I WOULD FOLLOW THEE

#220 LDS Hymn Book 1985 Edition

Susan Evans McCloud and K. Newell Dayley

Copyright 1985 LDS Church

Music only; Background for Ryan's narration

Scene Four: **TEACH ME TO WALK IN THE LIGHT**

#177 LDS Children's Songbook 2014 Edition

Clara McMaster

Copyright 1958, 1986 LDS Church

Sung by Children's Chorus: Scene Opener

A POOR WAYFARING MAN OF GRIEF

#29 LDS Hymn Book 1985 Edition

James Mongomery and George Coles

Music only; Background for King Benjamin's Vision

MARY'S LULLABY

#44 LDS Children's Songbook 2014 Edition

Jan Underwood Pinborough and Darwin Wolford

Sung by Mary, acapella, to baby Jesus

Scene Seven: **BOOK OF MORMON STORIES**

#118 LDS Children's Songbook 2014 Edition

Elizabeth F. Bates

Copyright 1969, 1986 LDS Church

Fourth Verse sung by Children's Chorus: Scene Opener

Scene Eight: **BAPTISM**

#100 LDS Children's Songbook 2014 Edition

Mabel Jones Gabbott and Crawford Gates

Copyright 1969 LDS Church

Sung by Children's Chorus: Background for Scene

Scene Ten: **BOOK OF MORMON STORIES**

#118 LDS Children's Songbook 2014 Edition

Elizabeth F. Bates

Copyright 1969, 1986 LDS Church

Third Verse sung by Children's Chorus: Scene Opener

WHEN HE COMES AGAIN

#82 LDS Children's Songbook 2014 Editon

Mirla Greenwood Thayne

Copyright 1952, 1980

Music only; Background for Tracy's narration

Scene Thirteen: **BOOK OF MORMON STORIES**

#118 LDS Children's Songbook 2014 Edition

Elizabeth F. Bates

Copyright 1969, 1986 LDS Church

Fifth Verse sung by Children's Chorus: Scene Opener

Scene 13 and 14:	**WHERE LOVE IS**
	#138 LDS Children's Songbook 2014 Edition
	Joanne Bushman Doxey, Norma B. Smith, Marjorie Castleton Kjar
	Copyright 1972, Joanne Bushman Doxey, Marjorie Castleton Kjar
	Music only; Background for Holly's narration
Scene Sixteen:	**BOOK OF MORMON STORIES**
	#118 LDS Children's Songbook 2014 Edition
	Elizabeth F. Bates
	Copyright 1969, 1986 LDS Church
	Sixth Verse sung by Children's Chorus: Scene Opener
	GOD OF OUR FATHERS, WHOSE ALMIGHTY HAND
	#78 LDS Hymns 1985 Edition
	Daniel C. Roberts and George W. Warren
	Music only: Background for Ryan's narration
Scene Eighteen:	**BOOK OF MORMON STORIES**
	#118 LDS Children's Songbook 2014 Edition
	Elizabeth F. Bates
	Copyright 1969, 1986 LDS Church
	Seventh Verse sung by Children's Chorus: Scene Opener
	KEEP THE COMMANDMENTS
	#146 LDS Children's Songbook 2014 Edition
	Barbara A. McConochie
	Copyright 1975 LDS Church
	Sung by Children's Chorus, Post-scene
Scene Twenty:	**FEEL MY SAVIOUR'S LOVE**
	#74 LDS Children's Songbook 2014 Edition
	Ralph Rogers Jr., K. Newell Dayley, Laurie Huffman
	Copyright 1979, Sonos Music
	Music only; Background for Moroni's narration

PRODUCTION NOTES

In order to quickly and easily relocate dry ice, plants, and rocks for scene changes, one plant and one to three rocks should be placed on a dolly with a small bucket of dry ice hidden in the middle of them. This is referred to as a BPDIA on the charts and throughout the script; B stands for Boulders; P stands for Plant; DIA stands for Dry Ice Arrangement. For each bucket, you will need enough dry ice to vaporize for two to three hours. If possible, the platform should be covered with carpeting. When this is not possible, use area rugs.

It is recommended that an open auditorium, one in which seats must be set up, i.e., a gymnasium or cultural hall, as opposed to one with fixed seating, be used for this production to more easily facilitate the audience/actor interaction required throughout the play and specifically in scenes one, six, eight, thirteen, sixteen, eighteen, and twenty-two. If this is not possible, it will be necessary to keep vacant selected rows so as to allow the Hebrew Prophets, Abinadi, Ammon, Helaman and the Warriors, and Jesus to walk among the audience.

In addition to music, which can be piano or orchestra accompanied, a violin is needed for sound effects.

Scriptures and narrations which are read from cards need not be memorized. However, they must be rehearsed thoroughly to ensure smooth and flawless rendering.

DO NOT list the names of the actor and infant appearing as Jesus on the program. **DO NOT** introduce them to the audience or let the rest of the cast know who they are. This element of anonymity will assist the invitation of the spirit and strengthen the impact of the final scene. **PLEASE MAKE NO EXCEPTIONS ON THIS INSTRUCTION!**

IT IS ABSOLUTELY ESSENTIAL TO THE SUCCESS OF THE PRODUCTION, that the spirit of the final scene not be dispelled by curtain calls or applause. Therefore, if you wish to introduce your actors, do so before the play begins. A method of doing this is included in the opening remarks. Leave the audience in total darkness for a few moments after Jesus exits. They will revel in the spirit of what they have just experienced and applause will automatically be stifled.

OPENING REMARKS

It is essential to the success of the play, to the imparting of the intended message, that the spirit of the final scene not be disturbed by applause or curtain calls. Therefore, it is suggested that players are introduced prior to the commencement of the play in the following manner:

60 MINUTES PRIOR TO THE ANNOUNCED STARTING TIME OF THE PLAY

All cast members are to be in costume and make-up.

All fixed and initial props and scenery, including the Book of Mormon pages, are to be in place.

All doors to the auditorium, except one, are closed.

(Note: In case of emergency, all exits must still remain accessible. Therefore, for the purpose of seating your guests, direct them to the entrance selected for the audience use. Refer to Stage Chart - Auditorium, Audience Arrangement, and adapt for your auditorium.)

The house lighting is low.

Plants and rocks are in place as indicated on the Stage Chart – Auditorium, Audience Arrangement.

45   MINUTES PRIOR TO THE ANNOUNCED STARTING TIME OF THE PLAY

A medley of the music that will be used throughout the play begins to play softly.

So as to enhance the audience's ability to 'feel' the spirit of **THE FIRESIDE,** they are made part of the cast, part of the story, through the interactions which take place among them. Hence, they are guests at the fireside, and it is therefore important that ushers take their places at the entrance, and Wayne and Shannon Stewart take their places on the platform, which is arranged according to the Stage Chart – Platform, prior to the arrival of the first audience member.

Wayne is seated on a love-seat URC, reading a Liahona magazine. Shannon is dusting and arranging floor pillows and scriptures for their guests.

Wayne interrupts her several times to show her something in the Liahona.

Twice during the next fifteen minutes, at Shannon's request, Wayne leaves the platform and comes back, first with a pitcher of water and paper cups, then with napkins.

Shannon also leaves twice, first for a plate of refreshments, then for sheet music and a needlework project.

35 MINUTES PRIOR TO THE ANNOUNCED STARTING TIME OF THE PLAY

The choir assembles in front of the stage, directly across from the platform.

30 MINUTES PRIOR TO THE ANNOUNCED STARTING TIME OF THE PLAY

The choir begins the Prelude Songs. A white spotlight is on the choir, and a warm, amber or pink, spotlight is now on the platform.

Kellie enters the auditorium from behind the platform, carrying a set of keys and a bowl of snack mix. She steps up to the platform, R, and rings the doorbell.

Shannon greets her. She places the bowl on the living room table, next to the plate of refreshments, and her keys on the table next to the pillow; R. Kellie greets Wayne, then visits with Shannon.

Shannon shows Kellie her needlework project, tells her what she is doing, and allows her

Kellie to try some of it. Friendly conversation is exchanged, inaudible, to the arriving audience.

20 MINUTES PRIOR TO THE ANNOUNCED STARTING TIME OF THE PLAY

Daniel, Tracy, Heather, Laurel, and Holly enter the auditorium through the guest entrance, carrying:

> Daniel – a briefcase
>
> Tracy – a plate of cookies or brownies, a set of scriptures, and a purse
>
> Heather – two scrolls, a Liahona, a set of scriptures, and a purse
>
> Laurel – three sets of Gold Plates, a set of scriptures, and a purse
>
> Holly – one set of Gold Plates, one set of Brass Plates, and a set of scriptures

They step up to the Platform, and R. Daniel rings the doorbell. They are greeted by Wayne, and enter, in this order: Daniel, Holly, Heather, Laurel, then Tracy.

Wayne shows Daniel to the stool and music stand, ULC, where he helps Daniel arrange his notes and displays.

After giving the plates, scrolls and Liahona to Daniel, Heather, Laurel, and Holly introduce themselves to Kellie. Heather and Laurel continue to talk with her.

Holly goes to help Daniel.

Tracy places the plate of cookies or brownies on the living room table with the other refreshments and converses with Shannon.

All conversation is inaudible to the arriving audience.

15 MINUTES PRIOR TO THE ANNOUNCED STARTING TIME OF THE PLAY

Heather and Laurel sit down on the pillows C and begin reading.

Kellie joins Shannon and Tracy.

10 MINUTES PRIOR TO THE ANNOUNCED STARTING TIME OF THE PLAY

All cast members, except Platform actors, line up in the hall, just outside the guest entrance. Autumn, Ryan, and Amber enter the auditorium through the guest entrance. Autumn has a portfolio. Ryan has a Book of Mormon. Amber has a vase of cut flowers and a purse.

Ryan and Amber casually circle the auditorium. Autumn steps up to the platform, R, and rings the doorbell.

Shannon greets them, at which time Kellie sits on a pillow, R, by the love seat and Tracy seats herself L.

As soon as Heather sees Autumn, she goes to greet her and introduces her to the others. Autumn is seated by Tracy on the chair DL, and Heather moves to a pillow beside Autumn, DLC. Holly now takes the pillow Heather had been using, pulls it closer to Daniel, and sits down.

Tracy, Autumn, and Heather converse with each other.

Laurel is still reading.

Holly fiddles with the plates, scrolls, and Liahona.

Shannon converses with Kellie, who has gone back to the needlework.

Daniel and Wayne continue to converse.

All conversation is inaudible to the arriving audience.

5 MINUTES PRIOR TO THE ANNOUNCED STARTING TIME OF THE PLAY

Ryan and Amber step up to the Platform and ring the bell. Shannon greets them.

Autumn takes Heather over to meet them and introduces them to everyone else.

Shannon takes the vase and puts it on the table behind Daniel.

Ryan places his book on a seat DR, and Amber places her purse on another seat DR.

Everyone engages in conversation.

All conversation is inaudible to the arriving audience.

AT PRECISELY THE ANNOUNCED STARTING TIME OF THE PLAY

AFTER the last song, a fanfare is sounded and, simultaneously, all the Platform actors freeze.

House lights go down. Prelude music ends. Spotlights go down on the Platform and the Choir. The Choir exits.

In the darkness the voice of the Director is heard, though the Director is not seen.

> **DIRECTOR: We live our lives better and are more successful in spreading the gospel when we feel the love our Heavenly Father has for us. Every human being learns much from the experiences of his or her life. The wise share what they learn, both with their own generation and the generations that follow.**
>
> **Throughout time, the greatest lessons learned by mankind were those in which Heavenly Father had a part. This remains true today. There are many in our own time who teach from the pages of theirs lives. From them, we learn valuable lessons, as our time is a time "unlike any other."**
>
> **However, we must not overlook the tremendous importance of the lessons of other generations.**
>
> **Because divine laws are eternal, the knowledge gained through their dealings with Heavenly Father, by the men and women living in the pages of the Book of Mormon or any other book of scripture, is as pertinent to our time as it was to their own.**
>
> (Footlights go up; Director enters in front of the curtain, R, with a stack of photos, crosses to the book; as each actor is introduced, the director puts his or her photo, in Sunday dress, on the left page, as the audience sees it; each actor, when introduced, enters C from behind the curtain, through the pages of the book, puts his or her character picture on the right page, as the audience sees it, and states his or her character name; multitude players may choose their own name from the Bible or the Book of Mormon; actors exit through the audience; pre-assigned multitude characters, Lehi and his family and the Hebrew Prophets take their place

among the audience)

From the pages of the Book of Mormon, our contemporaries come to life as these ancestors:

DIRECTOR	ACTOR
Actor's Name	Lehi
Actor's Name	Sariah
Actor's Name	Laman
Actor's Name	Lemuel
Actor's Name	King Benjamin
Actor's Name	Mary, the mother of Jesus
Actor's Name	Abinadi
Actor's Name	King Noah
Actor's Name	First Priest
Actor's Name	Second Priest
Actor's Name	Ammon
Actor's Name	First Servant
Actor's Name	Second Servant
Actor's Name	Samuel the Lamanite
Actor's Name	Moroni
Actor's Name	Jared
Actor's Name	Brother of Jared
Actor's Name	Hebrew Prophet
Actor's Name	Hebrew Prophet
Actor's Name	Hebrew Prophet
Actor's Name	Hebrew Prophet
Actor's Name	Hebrew Prophet
Actor's Name	Sam
Actor's Name	Nephi
Actor's Name	Laban
Actor's Name	Zoram

Actor's Name	Laban's Guard
Actor's Name	Laban's Guard
Actor's Name	Laban's Guard
Actor's Name	Joseph
Actor's Names	Hebrews
Actor's Name	Priest
Actor's Name	Priest
Actor's Name	Priest
Actor's Name	Priest
Actor's Name	Priest
Actor's Name	Priest
Actor's Name	Priest
Actor's Name	Priest
Actor's Name	Priest
Actor's Name	King Noah's Guard
Actor's Name	King Noah's Guard
Actor's Name	King Noah's Guard
Actor's Name	King Noah's Guard
Actor's Name	Alma
Actor's Name	Alma the Younger
Actor's Name	Son of Mosiah
Actor's Name	Son of Mosiah
Actor's Name	Son of Mosiah
Actor's Name	Son of Mosiah
Actor's Name	Lamanite Guard
Actor's Name	Lamanite Guard
Actor's Name	Lamanite Guard
Actor's Name	Lamoni's Servant
Actor's Name	Lamoni's Servant
Actor's Name	Helaman
Actor's Names	Twenty Warriors

Actor's Names	Jaredites
Actor's Names	The Multitudes
Actor's Names	Children's Chorus
Actor's Name	Choir

(footlights go down, white spotlight goes up, P. As the actors are introduced and their pictures are placed on the book, they take their places on their chairs and pillows and resume inaudible conversation)

Their stories will be shared with us through these descendants:

Actor's Name	Wayne
Actor's Name	Shannon
Actor's Name	Daniel
Actor's Name	Tracy
Actor's Name	Heather
Actor's Name	Laurel
Actor's Name	Holly
Actor's Name	Autumn
Actor's Name	Ryan
Actor's Name	Amber
Actor's Name	Kellie

I will leave them now to introduce themselves and share with us some beautiful stories from the past.

(Director exits in front of the curtain, R. After opening prayer, the book is removed from the proscenium, behind the curtain, through backstage exits and the guest entrance, to the back of the auditorium, labeled pictures of the production crews are added)

SCENE ONE

WAYNE: (rises, crosses to C, simple gestures indicate he has never conducted and is nervous) **Well . . . I guess we should get started. Let's see . . .** (Shannon picks up the sheet music, hands it to him) **. . . oh, yes! We will begin with an opening song and prayer. The song is, SEARCH, PONDER, AND PRAY.** (he passes around the music) **After that we will have** (pauses as he looks overcast and audience; he makes his (pre-designated) selection from the audience) **Brother/Sister . . . , will offer the prayer.**

(low house lights up; Shannon steps down off the platform and stands in front of the audience to lead the music; after the song, she returns to her seat)

"GUEST:" (rises and moves in front of audience; offers prayer, then returns to seat; house lights go down; spotlight on P changes from white to amber of pink, hereafter spotlight on P is always amber or pink)

WAYNE: (rises, moves up; nervously) **I want to begin by thanking you for coming. Shannon and I really appreciate you being here tonight.** ("THE LORD IS MY SHEPHERD" begins playing softly in the background) **As some of you know, my wife and I have been members of The Church of Jesus Christ of Latter-Day Saints now for almost a year. I cannot begin to tell you how much this church means to us. I know you have probably heard that from every convert you have ever met. Maybe,** (directing his words to Daniel's family) **you have said it yourself. But please, believe me when I tell you that we are most sincere.**
You see... like everyone, I guess, ...we had our problems. But some of those problems were quite overwhelming. They were almost more than we could handle and we were just about to give up on a lot of things... maybe even each other. That was when the missionaries knocked on our door. (becoming a little more emotional) **Now, we were happy with our own church and we were NOT the kind of people who let strangers into our home, but that night . . . well . . . to be honest . . . we had just had an argument and would rather have talked to anyone but each other.** (Shannon smiles with recollection; guests chuckle) **They started asking us questions like, 'Have you ever thought about why we exist and what the purpose of this life really is?' Of course, we had! Maybe everyone does, but we did not know there were any answers to those questions. We laughed a little, at their questions until we began to realize they were answering them, and what they were saying was making sense. We felt something that night – something we had never felt before – and it felt good! So. . . when the elders asked if they could return, we, of course, said yes.**

43

It did not take many visits to see that the message these boys were sharing with us was something we desperately needed. We enjoyed every meeting we had with them and always learned something that helped us with our problems. And that wonderful feeling, which we learned was the Spirit of the Lord was always there.

We were so grateful to those boys for the happiness they were bringing to us, that we probably would have done anything for them. But when they invited us to be baptized, it was because of this (picks up a Book of Mormon) **the Book of Mormon that we said yes.**

They had given it to us that first night and asked us to read it, and to consider the testimony that was in it. (opens back cover of the book)

We knew right away that the book was true. But it was this man's testimony (points to writing in the book) **that . . . touched us in such a way . . . that we felt we just had to do as Moroni said** (turns to marked passage) **to "ask God, the Eternal Father, in the name of Christ, if these things are not true, and if ye shall ask with a sincere heart, with real intent, having faith in Christ, He will manifest the truth of it unto you, by the power of the Holy Ghost. And by the power of the Holy Ghost, ye may know the truth of all things."**

We wanted everything the missionaries had been teaching us to be true, and we wanted to know for ourselves that it was. As you have probably figured out, we did learn that these things are true. Now, that we know they are, we want to share them with others. (music ends) **That is why we have invited all of you here tonight.**

Now, I have said enough. It was the testimony of Daniel's family that impressed us, so we have asked them to share that testimony with you too. (returns to his seat)

DANIEL: (looking over the guests) **I see some unfamiliar faces. They are nice faces, and I would like to know the names that go with them. So, I will begin, we will pick up these three** (indicates Heather, Holly, and Laurel), **then go around this way** (indicates a counter-clockwise movement), **and introduce ourselves. I am Daniel Taylor. By profession, I am an architect, by providence, the father of three teenage daughters.**
(the guest chuckles and Tracy smiles, and the girls respond with . . .)

HEATHER: **Ha! Ha!**
LAUREL: **Cute, Daddy! Cute!**
HOLLY: **Very funny!**

HOLLY: **I am Holly Taylor. By profession, I am a student; by providence, the daughter of a comedian.** (more chuckles are her; Daniel smiles, Tracy shakes her head)

44

LAUREL: **I am Laurel Taylor. By profession, I am a high school senior; by providence, I also belong to him.** (points to Daniel, as he smile broadly with 'pride'; Tracy shakes her head even more)

HEATHER: **I am Heather Taylor. By providence . . . well, you know the joke, and** (directing her world to Daniel) **by tomorrow, at this time, I will no longer be a teenager.**

DANIEL: (playfully) **Oh, that is right! At somewhere around 3:00 in the morning, she will become a grand old lady of 20.**

HEATHER: (playfully, as if wounded) **Grand, yes, Daddy, but not old, and it is 3:40 a.m., to be precise.**

DANIEL: (with playful surrender) **Forgive me!**

TRACY: (still shaking her head and smiling, with a jovial tone in her voice) **They never stop!**
I am Tracy Taylor, wife and mother, and (indicating, with a small area sweep, Daniel, Heather, Laurel, and Holly) **manager of this act!**
(the girls respond with a playful expression of offense; Daniel just smiles with amusement)

(everyone has smiles on their faces and continues the introduction with pleasantness in their voices)

AUTUMN: **My name is Autumn McKay, and I work with Heather at Robert's Law Firm.**
She gave me one of those books, too (points to Wayne's Book of Mormon) **I cannot say that I have read it yet, but I did take a quick look at it, and I am quite curious about what is in it. So, when Heather told me about this fireside and invited me to come, I thought . . . why not, and said okay. So, here I am!**

AMBER: **Autumn has not been able to read her Book of Mormon because we have it. She showed it to me a few days after Heather gave it to her and said I could take a look at it while she was at work. I show it to Ryan that night, and we became so caught up in it that we never returned it.**

DANIEL: **Now that is the kind of problem I like to hear about, and** (pauses, as he reaches into his briefcase and pulls out a Book of Mormon) **I have the perfect solution for it.** (hands the book to Autumn)

AUTUMN: (with excited expression, as she receives the book) **Thank you!!**

RYAN: **I am Ryan Perry, Amber's husband. We are friends of the McKay family and came with them tonight because, as Autumn indicated, we are very intrigued by the Book of Mormon and want to know more about it.**

KELLIE: **My name is Kellie Haydon. I clean house for the Taylors and have known them for several years now. It used to be that I did not like working for them. They were always cranky and disagreeable and . . . well . . . just plain hard to get along with.** (Wayne nods his head, a little embarrassed; Shannon drops her face in her hands, guests react with mild shock and disbelief)
But, about a year ago, I began to notice a change in them. They argued less, became easier to please, and seemed to appreciate my work; Shannon even began helping me with some of the bigger chores. They were obviously happier.
Then, one afternoon, a few months ago, we were folding laundry, and my curiosity got the best of me. I asked her what had happened. That was all it took?
My two-word question seemed to have an endless answer. Every time I came to work, we would spend more time talking about the gospel and less time cleaning. I would go home and think about what she had said and come back with more questions.
When Wayne told me about this thing tonight, I invited myself.

SHANNON: **Wayne! I thought you invited her!!** (to Kellie) **Of course, you were invited!**

WAYNE: **I am Wayne Stewart, and this is my wife, Shannon. We are here . . . because this is our home . . .**

SHANNON: **Another comedian.**

WAYNE: **. . . and, yes, of course you were invited, Kellie, and all of you are welcome ~ anytime!**

DANIEL: **Okay!** (spreads his notes on the music stand) **Before I begin, I must ask for your help. This is a big topic, so, throughout the evening, I will be handling cards and marked scriptures to all of you to read. This should help everyone feel the spirit of the people of the Book of Mormon, and save me from losing my voice.**

LAUREL: (teasingly) **He really does that so no one will fall asleep.**

DANIEL: (to Laurel) **You get the first assignment.**
Now, as you all know, we are here tonight to talk about the Book of Mormon.

	In so doing, the first question we should answer is, 'What is the Book of Mormon?' Laurel, will you please read Ezekiel 37: 16, 17?
LAUREL:	(opens her BOM and reads Ezekiel 37: 16, 17) **"Moreover, thou son of man, take thee one stick and write upon it, For Judah,** (Daniel picks up one of the scrolls) **and for the children of Israel, his companions: then take another stick and write upon it, For Joseph,** (Daniel picks up the other scroll) **the stick of Ephraim, and for all the house of Israel, his companions: And join them one to another into one stick, and they shall become one in thine hand."**
DANIEL:	(holding the scrolls) **Thank you. In ancient times, record keeping was done on scrolls such as these. They were referred to as sticks. We know the Stick of Judah to be the Bible, but what is the Stick of Joseph?** (hands scrolls to Holly to pass around; when they return to Holly, she places them on display in front of the riser)
SHANNON:	(after a little silence) **The Book of Mormon**
DANIEL:	**That is right! Our records of God's dealings with man begin with Genesis. From Genesis to the reign of Zedekiah, King of Judah, all Israel shared the same history.** **Now, there was a lot of activity going on at the time of King Zedekiah's reign.** (low house lights go up, five Hebrew Prophets and Lehi arise from the audience and walk among the audience, preaching VERY quietly) **There were many prophets, preaching repentance to the people, and forewarning of the destruction of the city of Jerusalem, if they did not obey the Lord. One of those prophets was a man by the name of Lehi.** (spotlight on Lehi) **It was through Lehi that our Father in Heaven chose to preserve a portion of the tribe of Joseph in the Americas. Lehi, who was a descendent of Joseph, was directed by the Lord to leave Jerusalem and journey into the wilderness with his wife and children.** (Sariah, Laman, Lemuel, Sam, and Nephi arise from among the audience, convene with Lehi and follow him out of the auditorium DR; other prophets exit UR and UL; Children's Chorus enters quietly in front of the curtain, one-half form the L one half from the R, carrying Tom-Toms, meeting C, sit Indian style; behind the curtain, blue stage lights go up) **Before they had gone too far, he was directed by the Lord to send his sons back to Jerusalem to obtain the Plates of Brass from Laban.** (holds up Brass Plates, hands them down to be passed around and displayed, and at the same time, hands a card to Ryan) **This was a record of the Jews and a genealogy of their forefathers, the tribe of Joseph. It was similar to the Old Testament but more comprehensive.** (spotlight down)

SCENE TWO
OBTAINING THE BRASS PLATES OF LABAN

CHILDREN'S CHORUS: (footlights up) Sing **BOOK OF MORMON STORIES** verses one and two (when song has ended, children rise, exit in front of curtain, L and R, as curtain opens, footlights down)

SCENE: Lehi, Sariah, Laman, Lemuel, Sam, and Nephi are gathered around a campfire. Sariah is seated on a box, UR, of the campfire; Lehi is sitting cross-legged on the ground, DR, of the campfire; Laman, Lemuel, Sam, and Nephi are crouched around the campfire from UC to DL of the campfire, in that order from right to left. Over the left shoulder of Lemuel and right shoulder of Sam, behind the group, there is a BPDIA. URC and C there are two more BPDIA. ULC there is a Jerusalem house front. Two Guards stand on either side of the door. Laban sits on a large pillow between them with a third Guard crouched to his right. A BPDIA is over the right should of the guard, in front of the house.

NOTE: *All texts in quotes are taken directly from the Book of Mormon. While the location of the text is noted, in parentheses, at the end of the quote, it is not to be read!*

AT RISE: Laban and Guards are frozen. Lehi and his family are tending the fire and inter-acting with each other. When curtain is completely open, spotlight comes up on Lehi's family.

LEHI: **"Behold, I have dreamed a dream, in the which the Lord hath**

48

commanded me that thou and thy brethren shall return to Jerusalem. For behold, Laban hath the record of the Jews and also a genealogy of my forefathers, and they are engraven upon plates of brass. Wherefore, the Lord hath commanded me that thou and thy brothers should go unto the house of Laban and seek the records and bring them down hither into the wilderness." (I Nephi: 3: 2, 3, 4) (Laman and Lemuel murmur)

LAMAN & LEMUEL: (together murmur; suggested comments) **That is too hard a thing to ask of us! We cannot do that! How do you expect us to get the plates? Why do we need them, anyway?**

LEHI: (speaking to Nephi) **"Thy brothers murmur, saying it is a hard thing, which I have required of them. But I have not required it of them; it is a commandment of the Lord. Therefore, go, my son, and thou shalt be favored of the Lord because thou hast not murmured."** (I Nephi 3: 4, 5)

VOICE OF RYAN: (blue stage lights down, amber/red stage lights up; LORD, I WOULD FOLLOW THEE begins playing in the background; Laban and Guards come to life; Sariah and Lehi freeze; stage action follows narrative) **Nephi and his brothers did return to Jerusalem.** (exit DR, enter R, cross between BPDIA to C, crouch in circle, pantomiming the casting of lots) **They cast lots to determine who would go to Laban's house to get the brass plates. The lot fell to Laman.** (music ends, tension is created by the rapid bow action of a high cord on a violin and/or the repetitious striking of two low keys on a piano; Lemuel, Sam, and Nephi freeze behind BPDIA, C; Laman circles BPDIA, exits R, enters DR, crosses to LC) **He, alone, went to Laban's house. Laban was angry over his request, accused him of being a**

49

robber, and sought to kill him. (Laman quickly exits UR, enters R, crosses to BPDIA, C; Lemuel, Sam, and Nephi come to life) **Laman successfully escaped and returned to his brothers.** (tension effects end; LORD, I WOULD FOLLOW THEE resumes) **Laman and Lemuel wanted to return to their camp, but Nephi was determined to fulfill his commitment, and Sam was willing to do whatever the Lord had commanded.** (Lamen, Lemuel, Sam, and Nephi exit R) **They went back to the home they had left in Jerusalem to obtain their gold, silver, and other precious things, to offer in exchange for the brass plates.** (Laman, Lemuel, Sam, and Nephi enter R, with: Laman – three bags of gold, a silver tray, and a small box of jewels; Lemuel – three bags of gold, a pair of silver goblets, and a few ropes of jewels; Sam – five bags of gold, and a silver bowl; Nephi – three bags of gold, several ropes of jewels, and a box of spices) **Then, they returned to Laban's house together.** (music ends, tension effects begin; cross to LC) **Laban was very desirous to have the gold, silver, and precious things that Nephi and his brothers had to offer, but he was not willing to exchange the plates for them. Instead, he had his guards throw them out.** (Nephi and his brothers leave their possessions and flee, cross stage, exit R, enter UR, circle BPDIA, C, hide behind BPDIA, URC) **Then he sent his guards to kill them.** (Guards cross stage, exit R) **The guards were not successful and returned to Laban empty handed.** (Guards enter R, cross stage, are dismissed by an angry Laban, who holds a goblet in his left with a flask beside him, the guards exit L; Nephi emerges from BPDIA, circles BPDIA, C, exits UR, then enters R, (during this time, Laban, whose robe is on the ground beside him, begins to rise but falls down; this action is performed very quietly; his feet are upstage, in front of his house, with the empty goblet fallen from his hand; Nephi crosses to LC; tension effects end,

LORD, I WOULD FOLLOW THEE resumes) **Upon instruction from the Lord, Nephi returned to Jerusalem. He found Laban passed out on the street. The Spirit of the Lord directed him to kill Laban, but Nephi found that a difficult thing to do because he had never shed the blood of man. The Spirit of the Lord instructed him again to slay Laban, and said, "Behold, the lord slayeth the wicked to bring forth his righteous purposes. It is better that one man should perish than that a nation should dwindle and perish in unbelief "** (I Nephi 4: 13) **Nephi did as he was directed.** ('stabs' Laban, puts on Laban's garment, stands DLC, looking off-stage) **Dressed in the garments of Laban,** (Zoram enters DL with a large ring of keys) **he was able to obtain the brass plates from one of Laban's servants.** (Nephi follows Zoram off-stage L; they both return with Zoram holding the Brass Plates) **Nephi took Zoram with him back into the wilderness.** (Nephi and Zoram cross the stage, exit R, enter UR, circle BPDIA, C, stop RC; amber/red stage lights down, blue stage lights up; Sariah and Lehi come to life) **During the time Nephi and his brother had been gone, Sariah, Lehi's wife, had complained against her husband, because she was afraid her sons had been killed.**

SARIAH:	(deeply grieved) **"Behold, thou hast led us forth from the land of our inheritance, and my sons are no more, and we perish in the wilderness.** (I Nephi 5: 2) (Nephi, his brothers, and Zoram cross to campfire scene)
VOICE OF RYAN:	**When they returned, however, Sariah was greatly relieved and humbled, and her testimony had increased.**
SARIAH:	**"Now, I know of a surety that the Lord hath commanded my**

husband to flee into the wilderness; yea, and I also know of a surety that the Lord hath protected my sons, and delivered them out of the hands of Laban, and given them power whereby they could accomplish the thing which the Lord had commanded the." (I Nephi 5: 8) (music ends, curtain closes, stage light down)

SCENE THREE

DANIEL: (spotlight up, P) **Lehi's sons returned to Jerusalem one more time to persuade Ishmael and his household to join them.**

KELLIE: **Excuse me, who was Ishmael?**

TRACY: **Ishmael was a descendant of the tribe of Ephraim, the same as Lehi. The Lord knew that the lineage of Joseph could not have been continued through Lehi, if there had been no women for his sons to marry. So, he inspired Ishmael, with his wife, five daughters, and two sons, and their families to accompany Lehi's sons back into the wilderness.**

KELLIE: **Ohhh . . . that makes sense!**

DANIEL: **Their group, which now consisted of at least sixteen people, was guided through the wilderness by and instrument called the Liahona.** (holds up a model, then hands it to Tracy to be passed around and displayed) **The Liahona pointed the way for them to go, as long as they were faithful and believed the Lord would guide them. Heather, please read, I Nephi 16: 28 for us.**

HEATHER: **"And it came to pass that I, Nephi, beheld the pointers which were in the ball, that they did work according to the faith and diligence and heed which we did give unto them."**

DANIEL: **The Brass Plates of Laban were the first of the five sets of records which were compiled into the Book of Mormon. The next two sets of records were begun during their eight years journey in the wilderness**

53

and continued when they reached the Promised Land. They were the **Large and Small Plates of Nephi.** (holds up two sets of Gold Plates, then hands them to Tracy to be passed around and displayed; give Tracy a sheet of paper) **Tracy, will you read this?**

TRACY: (stands to read) **The Large Plates contained the record of Lehi from 590 B.C. to 570 B.C., the genealogy of Lehi's father, their experiences in the wilderness, a general secular record until 130 B.C., and a combined secular and sacred record from130 B.C. to 385 A.D. These were the official Nephite records as long as they were kept. The small plates contained spiritual events and many quotations from the Brass Plates of Laban. They were kept until King Benjamin began to record both secular and religious events on the Lare Plates.**

KELLIE: **Excuse me, again, please. Mr. Taylor, who was King Benjamin?**

DANIEL: **If you do not mind, I will get to him in a few minutes.** (Kellie's actions indicated that was ok) **When Lehi's group arrived at the seashore of the waters they called Irreantum, Nephi was directed to build a ship. When the ship was completed, they crossed the seas to the Promised Land, or what we now call South America. When they arrived, they found a land that was fertile, and contained gold and silver, an abundance of food, and many kinds of animals. Their needs were met and they began a new life. But, as it goes with people, it was not long before contentions separated them into two groups. Wayne, would you please real II Nephi 5: 1, 2, 5, & 6"**

WAYNE: **"Behold, it came to pass that I, Nephi, did cry much unto the Lord, my God, because of the anger of my brethren.**
"But behold, their anger did increase against me, insomuch that they did seek to take away my life.

54

"And it came to pass that the Lord did warn me, that I, Nephi, should depart from them, and flee into the wilderness, and all those who would go with me.

"Wherefore, it came to pass that I, Nephi did take my family and also Zoram and his family and Sam, mine elder brother, and his family and Jacob and Joseph, my younger brethren, and also my sisters, and all those who would go with me. And all those who would go with me were those who believed in the warnings and the revelations of God: wherefore, they did hearken unto my worlds."

DANIEL: Thank-you! All those who followed Nephi called themselves Nephites. They were a righteous people. Those who followed Laman and Lemuel called themselves Lamanites. They were wicked. Holly, will you please read II Nephi 5: 21 & 24

HOLLY: "And he had caused the cursing to come upon them, yea, even a sore cursing, because of their iniquity. For behold, they had hardened their hearts against him, that they had become like unto a flint; wherefore, as they were white and exceedingly fair and delightsome, that they might not be enticing unto my people, the Lord God did cause a skin of blackness to come upon them.

"And because of their cursing, which was upon them, they did become an idle people, full of mischief and subtlety, and did seek in the wilderness for beasts of prey."

DANIEL: Now, not all the Nephites remained righteous. As the years passed, and especially after the death of Nephi, some of them fell into iniquity and became as wicked as the Lamanites. God then directed a man named Mosiah to lead all the righteous Nephites to a land called Zarahemla. There they lived peacefully with a group of people, call the Mulekites. They too had come from Jerusalem. Mosiah was made their first king. When King Mosiah died, his son became king.

(directing his focus to Kellie) **His son was King Benjamin.** (behind curtain, blue stage lights up; multitudes enter auditorium DR, gather in front of stage R, and filter among the audience; **Children's Chorus** enters in front of curtain, one half, R, and one half, L, meeting C; sit cross-legged on the proscenium) **King Benjamin was a good king and a righteous man. He delivered an address to his people before his death which stirred them to repentance and righteous living.** (spotlight P, down)

SCENE FOUR
KING BENJAMIN SPEAKS TO HIS PEOPLE

CHILDREN'S CHORUS: (footlights up; dim house light up) Sing first verse of **TEACH ME TO WALK IN THE** LIGH)

ADULT MULTITUEDS: (sing second verse, of **TEACH ME TO WALK IN THE** LIGHT)

CHILDREN'S CHORUS AND ADULT MULTITUDES: (sing third verse; when song has ended children rise, exit DC to join multitude, footlights down, curtain opens, amber spotlight up on King Benjamin)

SCENE: King Benjamin is behind battle tower, elevated several feet off the stage floor, DL; a BPDIA is L of the tower; ULC to L there is a Jerusalem house front, before which stands a small group of men, women, and children, in need of healing; a BPCIA is behind the people, R of the house; Mary is seated on a bale of hay before a cradle C, holding Baby Jesus; Joseph is standing over her right shoulder; a BPDIA is behind them; a large boulder is DR, a BPDIA is behind and just R of the boulder

AT RISE: Living stories characters are frozen; King Benjamin is speaking

KING BENJAMIN: **My brethren, all ye that have assembled yourselves together, you that can hear my words which I shall speak unto you this day . . . I am like yourselves . . . yet I have been chosen by this people, and consecrated by my father, and was suffered by the hand of the Lord that I should be a ruler and a king over this people; and have been kept and preserved by his matchless**

power, to serve you with all the might, mind, and strength which the Lord hath granted unto me. . . . Behold . . . because I said unto you that I had spent my days in your service, I do not desire to boast, for I have only been in the service of God. And behold, I tell you these things that ye may learn wisdom; that ye may learn that when ye are in the service of your fellow beings ye are only in the service of your God.

I say unto you that if ye should serve Him who had created you from the beginning . . . and is with all your whole souls yet ye would be unprofitable servants.

And behold, all that He requires of you is to keep His commandments; and He has promised you that if ye would keep His commandments ye should prosper in the land. . . .

And again by brethren, I would call your attention, for behold, I have somewhat more to speak unto you concerning that which is to come. (A POOR WAYFARING MAN OF GRIEF begins to play in the background)

For behold the time commeth, and is not far distant, that with power, the Lord Omnipotent, who reigneth, who was, and is from all eternity to all eternity, shall come down from heaven among the children of men. (spotlight down on King Benjamin; up C, Mary, Joseph, and Baby Jesus come to life; stage action precedes narrative)

He shall be called Jesus Christ, the Son of God, the Father of Heaven and Earth, the Creator of all things from the beginning; and his mother shall be called Mary. (music ends; Mary sings **MARY'S LULLABY**, a capella; spotlight down on C, Mary, Joseph, and Baby Jesus quietly exit UR; A POOR WAYFARING MAN OF GRIEF resumes; spotlight up LC; Jerusalem group comes to life; Jesus enters, L)

He shall go forth amongst men, working mighty miracles, such as healing the sick, raising the dead, causing the lame to walk, the blind to receive their sight, and the deaf to hear, and curing all manner of diseases.

And he shall cast our devils, or the evil spirits which dwell in the hearts of children of men. (spotlight down, Jesus exits UL, crosses behind backdrop; enters R, kneels at large boulder; Jerusalem group quietly exits UL)

And lo, He shall suffer temptations and pain of body, hunger, thirst and fatigue, even more than man can suffer, except it be unto death; for behold, blood cometh from every pore, so great shall be His anguish for the wickedness and the abominations of his people. (spotlight up, DR)

And lo, He cometh unto His own, that salvation might come unto the children of men even through faith on His name; and even after all this they shall consider Him a man and say that He hath a devil and shall crucify Him,

And He shall rise the third day from the dead; (Jesus rises) and behold, He standeth to judge the world; and behold, all these things are done that a righteous judgment might come upon the children of men. (spotlight down DR; Jesus exits DR; spotlight up on King Benjamin, music ends)

For the natural man is an enemy to God and has been from the fall of Adam, and will be forever and ever, unless he yields to the enticing of the Holy Spirit and becometh as a child, submissive, meek, humble, patient, full of love, willing to submit to all things which the Lord seeth fit to inflict upon him, even as a child doth submit to his father.

And now I have spoken the words which the Lord God hath commanded me.

And thus, saith the Lord: They shall stand as a bright testimony against this people at the judgment day; wherefore they shall be judged, every man according to his works, whether they be good or whether they be evil. (spotlight and stage lights down; curtains close; multitudes exit auditorium DR) (Mosiah 2: 9, 11, 16, 17, 21, 22 and Mosiah 3: 1, 5, 6, 7, 8, 9, 10, 19, 23, 24)

SCENE FIVE

DANIEL: (spotlight up, P) **There was a great conversion of the people, which led them to repent and live in righteousness. Some of the people went back to the city of Nephi and continued to live in righteousness until Noah, the son of Zeniff, became king. The people then became wicked again because King Noah was a wicked man, who chose wicked men to lead the church. So, of course, the people were taught to sin.** (dim house lights go up) **God sent a prophet named Abinadi to call the people to repentance.** (hands cards to Amber and Autumn; spotlight down, P)

SCENE SIX
ABINADI WARNS THE PEOPLE

ABINADI: (tension is created by the rapid bow action of a high cord on a violin and/or the repetitious striking of two low keys on a piano; enters the auditorium UL, red spotlight up on Abinadi; it follows him through audience and out of the auditorium DR)

Thus has the Lord commanded me, saying . . . Abinadi, go and prophesy unto this my people, for they have hardened their hearts against my words; they have repented not of their evil doing; therefore, I will visit them in my anger, yea, in my fierce anger will I visit them in their iniquities and abominations.

It shall come to pass that this generation, because of their iniquities, shall be smitten with a great pestilence. I will utterly destroy them from off the face of the earth; yet they shall leave a record behind them and I will preserve them for other nations which shall possess the land, that I may discover the abominations of this people to other nations. (Children's Chorus enters in front of curtain, one half, R and one half, L, carrying tom-toms; meeting C, sit cross-legged on the proscenium) **And it shall come to pass that the life of King Noah shall be valued even as a garment in a hot furnace; for he shall know that I am the Lord.** (house lights down; footlights up; behind curtain, red stage lights up)

SCENE SEVEN
ABINADI WARNS KING NOAH

CHILDREN'S CHORUS: (tension effects end) sing **BOOK OF MORMON STORIES**, verse four (children rise; exit in front of curtain L, and R, as curtain opens, tension effects resume)

SCENE: A low wall crosses the stage in front of the back-drop; a box for the priests is in front of the wall, C to L; two BPDIA are at either side of the box; RC is King Noah's throne, where he is seated with a goblet in one hand and grapes in the other; one priest, standing UL of him, is talking with him, the other priests are in conversation with each other around the stage; a BPDIA is DR and slightly behind King Noah's throne, another BPDIA is DL

AT RISE: Abinadi, in chains, is brought in DLC by two guards; priests enter The Priest Box, with one remaining beside King Noah, over his left shoulder

VOICE OF AMBER: (as curtain opens) **King Noah was extremely angry when he heard of Abinadi's prophecies. He ordered Abinadi to be brought to him, with intent to trick him, so that they could find cause to put him to death.**

FIRST PRIEST: (King Noah motions for questioning to begin) **What meaneth the words which are written, . . .**
How beautiful upon the mountains are the feet of him that bringeth good tidings; that publisheth peace; . . . that publisheth salvation; that saith unto Zion, Thy God reigneth?

ABINABAI:	Are you priests and pretend to teach this people and to understand the spirit of prophesying and yet desire to know of me what these things mean? What teach ye this people?
SECOND PRIEST:	We teach the law of Mosel
ABINADI:	If ye teach the law of Moses, why do ye not keep it? (priests, excepting one (Alma) begin to exhibit defensive, nervous actions) Why do ye set your heart upon riches, commit whoredoms, spend your strength with harlots, and cause this people to sin? Ye shall be smitten for your iniquities.
KING NOAH:	(angrily) Away with this fellow and slay him; for what have we to do with him, for he is mad.
ABINADI:	Touch me not, for God shall smite you if ye lay your hands upon me, for I have not delivered the message which the Lord sent me to deliver; therefore, God will not suffer that I shall be destroyed at this time.
	I finish my message, then it matters not whither I go, if it so be that I am saved. But this much I tell you, what you do with me, after this, shall be as a type and a shadow of things which are to come. And now I read unto you the remainder of the commandments of God:
	Thou shalt not make unto thee any graven image, nor serve Them. Thou shalt not take the name of the Lord thy God in vain. Remember the sabbath day, to keep it holy.
	Honor thy father and thy mother. Thou shalt not kill.
	Thou shalt not commit adultery. Thou shalt not steal.
	Thou shalt not bear false witness against thy neighbor.
	Thou shalt not covet thy neighbor's house, wife, nor anything

that is thy neighbor's.

Have ye taught this people that they should observe to do all these things? I say unto you, Nay; for if ye had, the Lord would not have caused me to come forth and to prophesy evil concerning this people.

And now, ought ye not to tremble and repent of your sins and remember that only in and through Christ ye can be saved? Therefore, if ye teach the law of Moses, also teach that it is a shadow of those things which are to come – who is the very Eternal Father. Amen (Mosiah 12: 20, 21, 25, 27, 28, 29, 31 and Mosiah 13: 1, 2, 3, 7, 9, 26 and Mosiah 16: 13, 14, 15)

VOICE OF AUMUMN: **King Noah put Abinadi to death by fire,** (guards drag Abinadi out L) **and later dies the same way.** (tension effects stop abruptly; stage lights down; Alma, leaving his priest garment behind him, exits C, to Waters of Mormon, which are brought in with the multitudes, auditorium DR; multitudes filter through audience; a BPDIA is placed R of waters; curtains close) **Only one of the priest believed Abinadi's words, repented and went on to become a great spiritual leader; that was Alma. Many people followed him and were baptized in the Waters of Mormon. Alma became the leader of the church in Zarahemla and taught the people in righteousness.**

SCENE EIGHT
ALMA BAPTIZES HIS PEOPLE

CHILDREN'S CHORUS: (enters in front of curtain, one half R, and one half L; meet C, sit cross-legged on the proscenium; footlights up; blue spotlight up on Waters of Mormon)

Sings **BAPTISM** (some of the multitude are being baptized by Alma during the song; at conclusion of song, spotlight and footlights down; multitudes and waters exit auditorium DR)

SCENE NINE

DANIEL: (amber or pink spotlight up, P) **There were those, however, who did not follow Alma's teachings. One of them was his own son, Alma the Younger. Alma the Younger and four sons of King Mosiah led many people away from the church in an attempt to destroy it, until a miraculous conversion took place. Tracy is going to read to us the account of that event from Mosiah 27.** (spotlight down)

SCENE TEN
THE CONVERSION OF ALMA THE YOUNGER AND THE FOUR SONS OF MOSIAH

CHILDREN'S CHORUS: (Children's Chorus enters, on half R, and one half L, carrying tom-toms; meet C, sit cross-legged on the proscenium; footlights up) Sings **BOOK OF MORMON STORIES**, verse three; exits L, and R, as curtain opens

SCENE: BPDIA are DRC, UC, UR, and L; Alma, kneeling, is frozen in front of a cot DL

AT RISE: Alma the Younger and the sons of Mosiah enter DR, cross to C; WHEN HE COMES AGAIN begins playing in the background

TRACY: (stage action precedes narrative; DO NOT USE ANY LIGHTING OR SPECIAL SOUND EFFECTS FOR THE ANGEL) **As they were going about rebelling against God, behold, the angel of the Lord appeared unto them; and he descended as it were in a cloud; and he spake as it were with a voice of thunder, which caused the earth to shake upon which they stood; And so great was their astonishment, that they fell to the earth and understood not the words which he spake unto them. Nevertheless, he cried again, saying:** (Mosiah 27: 11, 12, 13)

ANGEL: (amplified voice from off stage) **"Alma, arise and stand forth,** (pause, Alma rises slowly to his feet, facing back stage, looking up; the sons of Mosiah rise even more slowly, only to their knees, shielding their eyes) **for why persecutes thou the church of**

God? For the Lord hath said: This is my church and I will establish it; and nothing shall overthrow it, save it is the transgression of my people

Behold, the Lord hath heard the prayers of his people, and also the prayers of his servant, Alma, who is thy father; for he has prayed with much faith concerning thee that thou mightiest be brought to the knowledge of the truth; therefore, for this purpose have I come to convince thee of the power and authority of God, that the prayers of his servants might be answered according to their faith.

And now, behold, can ye dispute the power of God? (Alma and the sons of Mosiah tremble) For behold, doth not my voice shake the earth: And can ye not also behold me before you? And I am sent from God.

Now, I say unto thee: Go, . . . and seek to destroy the church no more, that their prayers may be answered, and even if thou wilt, of thyself be cast off. (Alma the Younger and the sons of Mosiah fall as if thrush down) (Mosiah 27: 13, 14, 15, 16)

TRACY:

And now Alma and those that were with him fell again to the earth for great was their astonishment. (pause, the sons of Mosiah begin to rise; notice Alma has not risen; attempt to stir him)

And now the astonishment of Alma was so great that he became dumb, yeas and he became weak; therefore, he was taken by those that were with him and carried helpless, even until he was laid before his father. (Alma come to life)

And they rehearsed unto his father all that had happened; and his father rejoiced for he knew that it was the power of God."

(music ends; stage lights down; curtains close)

(Mosiah 27: 18, 19, 20)

SCENE ELEVEN

DANIEL: (spotlight up, P) **After Alma the Younger recovered, both he and the Sons of Mosiah became missionaries for the church and went to preach the gospel to both Nephites and Lamanites. Many people of both groups were converted through their efforts. For example: through Ammon, the people of Lamoni accepted the gospel and joined the church.** (behind curtains, amber stage lights up; curtains open) **Here, Holly.** (Daniel hands a card to Holly; spotlight down, P)

SCENE TWELVE
AMMON'S MISSION TO THE LAMANITE COUNTRY

SCENE: There is a low wall U, from UR to UL; King Lamoni's throne is LC; R and L and slightly behind the throne are BPDIA; RC and DR are BPDIA; a runner extends downstage from the throne

AT RISE: King Lamoni is seated in his throne with guards on either side of him; Ammon is standing at the end of the runner, facing King Lamoni, with guards on either side of him

HOLLY: **When Ammon went to the Land of Ishmael to preach the gospel to the Lamanites, he was bound and taken before King Lamoni.**

KING LAMONI: **Is it your desire to dwell in this land among the Lamanites?**

AMMON: **Yea, I desire to dwell among this people for a time; yea, and perhaps until the day I die.**

KING LAMONI: (to the guards) **Loose his bands.** (the guards remove then bands from Ammon; after studying Ammon for a few moments) **I would that you should take one of my daughters to wife.**

AMMON: **Nay, but I will be thy servant.**

KING LAMONI: **Set him with the other servants to watch my flocks.** (Ammon and the two guards exit DR, stage lights down, as curtains close; Children's Chorus enters R and L in front of the curtain, carrying tom-toms, meet C, sit cross-legged on the proscenium)

SCENE THIRTEEN
AMMON AT THE WATERING PLACE

CHILDREN'S CHORUS: Sing **BOOK OF MORMON STORIES,** verse five (exit, one half R and one half L; footlights down)

SCENE: Low house lights up; tension is created by the rapid bow action of a high cord on a violin and/or the repetitious striking of two low keys on a piano; Ammon and two servants enter auditorium UL with several sheep; they herd the sheep through audience to DC

HOLLY: **When Ammon and the king's servants were driving the king's flocks to a place of water, other Lamanites scattered the flocks.** (four Lamanite servants enter DR and chase the sheep UC; stage hands contain the sheep in the auditorium) **The servants were fearful and wept.**

FIRST SERVANT: **Now the king will slay us, as he has our brethren because their flocks were scattered by the wickedness of these men.**

SECOND SERVANT: **Behold, our flocks are scattered already.** (tension effect gradually end; WHERE LOVE IS begins to play in the background)

HOLLY: (action slightly precedes narration) **Ammon comforted and encouraged the servants and together they gathered the flocks.** (Ammon and the servants herd the sheep back to DCR; ten servants, with clubs, enter UL) **When the wicked men again came to scatter their flocks, Ammon told the servants to encircle the animals, and he went to confront the men.** (music

72

ends; tension effects resume) **Now, of course, these men did not fear Ammon, because there was only one Ammon and there were many of them. But, by the power of God, Ammon was able to stand against them.** (picks up stones from among those put down with the scenery) **He slew six of them with stones,** (two servants fall to the ground) **and their leader with a sword. He smote off the arms of all who raised a club to smite him.** (four servants fall so as to leave only one arm visible) **When they saw that they could not defeat Ammon, the wicked servants fled.** (three servants exit at a run DR; tension effects end; music

resumes) **Ammon returned to help water the flocks.** (house lights down; stage lights up; curtains open as Ammon, servants and sheep exit Dr) **When King Lamoni heard of this matter, he called for Ammon.**

(conversation words for all speakers taken from, but not all exact, Mosiah 17: 27, 28, 32, 33, 35, 36, 37

SCENE FOURTEEN
AMMON TEACHES KING LAMONI

SCENE: The throne room of scene twelve.

AT RISE: Ammon enters DR; stands at end of runner

AMMON: **What wilt thou that I should do for thee, O King?** (Mosiah 18: 14)

KING LAMONI: **Tell me by what power ye slew and smote off the arms of my brethren that scattered my flocks.** (Mosiah 18: 20)

AMMON: **Believest thou that there is a God?** (Mosiah 18; 24)

KING LAMONI: **I do not know what thou meaneth?** Mosiah 18: 25)

AMMON: **Believest thou that there is a Great Spirit?** (Mosiah 18: 26)

KING LAMONI: **Yea.** (Mosiah 18: 27)

HOLLY: (action follows the narration) **Ammon began at the creation of the world and told Lamoni all the things concerning the holy scriptures, the journeyings of Lehi, the rebellions of Lamam and Lemuel, the Plan of Redemption, the coming of Christ, and all the works of the Lord. Lamoni received all of the words of Ammon. He asked Ammon to teach his people.** (Lamanites enter DR and DL; Ammon teaches among them) **Through Ammon's teaching, many were converted and baptized and a church was organized.** (spotlight up on P; curtains close; stage lights down)

SCENE FIFTEEN

DANIEL: There were still many Lamanites who did not accept the gospel. In their wickedness they sought to destroy those who had been converted. The Nephites fought to protect the people of Ammon.

AUTUMN: Wait! The people of Ammon? I thought we were talking about King Lamini's people.

HEATHER: We are. Because the wicked Lamanites were murdering King Lamoni's people, Ammon took them back to the Land of Zarahemla. They were given the Land of Jershon and became known as the people of Ammon. The Nephites protected them from their enemies.

AUTUMN: Why didn't they defend themselves?

HEATHER: When they gained their testimonies, they felt really bad for having killed so many Nephites. So, they took and oath to never shed blood again, even in their own defense. They knew that the wicked Lamanites would kill them, and there were many who did die, but they had made a promise to God, which they took seriously, and did not want to break.

RYAN: It is great that they were so repentant, but did not they feel guilty letting the Nephites die for them? I assume some Nephites did die?

LAUREL: Yes, some Nephites did die, and the people of Ammon did feel bad. So much so, that they were willing to break their oath and fight to defend themselves. But Helaman would not let them. He felt it was more important for them to keep their promise to Heavenly Father. (Children's Chorus enters, one half R and one half L, in front of the curtain, carrying tom-toms, meet C; sit cross-legged on the proscenium; behind curtains amber stage lights up; Laurel hands open Book of Mormon to Ryan) **Here, read what my dad marked in these verses of Alma 53.**

SCENE SIXTEEN
HELAMAN AND THE STRIPLING WARRIORS

CHILDREN'S CHORUS: Sings **BOOK OF MORMON STORIES,** verse six; exits, one half R and one half L; as curtain opens, fanfare, GOD OF OUR FATEHRS, WHOSE ALMIGHTY HAND begins playing in the background)

SCENE: BPDIA are located DR, URC, ULC, and DL; a large group covers the stage; there are piles of knives, swords, spears, and shields U) (Verses read: Alma 53: 13, 14, 16, 18, 19, 20, 22)

AT RISE: Helaman is talking with them

RYAN: (stage action precedes narration) **It came to pass that when they saw the danger and the many afflictions and tribulations which the Nephites bore for them, they were moved with compassion and were desirous to take up arms in the defense of their country. But they were overpowered by the persuasions of Helaman and his brethren. They had many sons who had not entered into a covenant that they would not defend themselves against their enemies; therefore, they did assemble themselves together at this time and they called themselves Nephites.** (Helaman selects Twenty Warriors to represent the 2000 Warriors; lines them up in two columns, DRC to URC, and DLC to ULC, facing audience and across UR and UL)

Now, behold, there were two thousand of those young men and they would that Helaman should be there leader. (Helaman gives knives, swords, spears, and shields to warriors)

They were all young men and they were exceedingly valiant for courage and also for strength. They were true at all times to whatsoever thing they were entrusted. (Helaman takes his place in front of the columns; mounts horse)

Helaman did march at the head of his 2000 Stripling Warriors. (Helaman raises his sword; fanfare; dim house lights up; warriors raise their spears; exit, marching D, down steps, down center aisle to back of auditorium; curtain begins to close slowly as soon as last warrior has crossed curtain line; stage lights down; Helaman stops; faces stage; marks time; warriors split - right column, as facing Helaman, exits auditorium UL; left column, as facing Helaman, exits auditorium UR; Helaman exits DR after last warrior passes him; house light down; music ends)

SCENE SEVENTEEN

DANIEL: (spotlight up, P) **These young men won their battle. Though all of them were sick or hurt, not a one of them had been killed.**

AMBER: **I am a little confused. You said these people who took this oath not to fight were Lamanites. So, the Nephites were defending them. If the Lamanites and the Nephites were on the same side, who were they fighting?**

DANIEL: **They were fighting the wicked Lamanites. There were periods of time when the Nephites were righteous and the Lamanites were wicked. There were times when there was a mixture of righteousness and wickedness among both groups. There were also times when pretty nearly all the Nephites were wicked. Such a condition existed just six years before the Savior's birth. As a matter of fact, it was a Lamanite prophet by the name of Samuel who was sent to call the Nephites to repentance.** (behind curtains, blue stage lights up; multitudes enter auditorium UL, UR, and DR with stones; gather in front of stage and through audience) **When Samuel went to warn the Nephites, they would not even let him into their city. He had to preach to them from atop the city wall.** (spotlight down, P)

SCENE EITHTEEN
SAMEIL THE LAMANITE WARNS THE NEPHITES

CHILDREN'S CHORUS: (footlights up, enter in front of curtain, one half, R and one half, L, carrying tom-toms, meet C, sit cross-legged on the proscenium) Sings **BOOK OF MORMON STORIES,** verse seven (children exit R and L, as curtain opens three quarters full to reveal RC to LC section; red spotlight up C; tension is created by the rapid bow action on a high cord on the violin and/or by the repetitious striking of two low keys on the piano)

SCENE: A city wall, RC to LC, BPDIA are on either side of and behind the wall; the curtains align with the BPDIA

AT RISE: Samuel the Lamanite is on the city wall, holding a staff, arms outstretched; delivering his exhortation; the multitudes are throwing stones at him;

Note: the stones they throw are not real stones; they are fake stones made our of paper

MULTITUDES MUST MISS SAMUEL WITH THEIR STONES! HE CANNOT BE HIT!!!!!!!!!!!!!!!!!!!!!!!!!!!!!!!!!!!

SAMUEL THE LAMANITE: Behold, I, Samuel, a Lamanite, do speak the words of the Lord which He doth put into my heart; and behold He hath put it into my heart to say unto this people that the sword of justice hangeth over this people; four hundred years pass not away save the sword of justice falleth upon this people. And nothing can save this people save it be repentance and

faith on the Lord Jesus Christ, who surely shall come into the world. (Samuel jumps down behind the wall, exits UL; tension effects end; red spotlight down; Children's Chorus return to proscenium as curtain closes; stage light down; footlights up)

CHILDREN'S CHORUS: Sings **KEEP THE COMMANDMENTS** (multitudes exit auditorium DR; footlights down; children exit in front of curtain R and L)

SCENE NINETEEN

DANIEL: (amber or pink spotlight, P) **Some of the Nephites did repent, many did not. And eventually, Samuel's prophesy came to pass; all the Nephites were destroyed.**

AUTUMN: **If they were all destroyed, where did the records for the Book of Mormon come from?**

DANIEL: **Shannon, we have talked about this before; why don't you answer Autumn's question?**

SHANNON: **Oh . . . hmmm . . . okay, I can do that. The Plates of Nephi had been passed down for generations through righteous men whom God trusted. Sometime before all the Nephites were destroyed, a man named Ammaron gave those plates to Mormon. Mormon made an abridgment of the Large Plates of Nephi, attached the Small Plate of Nephi to that abridgment, and added his own records. They were called the Plates of Mormon.** (Daniel holds up another set of Gold Plates, hands them Shannon to be passed around and displayed) **He gave them to his son Moroni. Moroni added his account and included an abridgment of the Plates of Ether.** (Daniel holds up the last set of Gold Plates; hands them to Shannon to be passes around and displayed) **When he was the only Nephite left, he buried the plates in the Hill Cumorah.**

WAYNE: **And that is where they stayed until that same Moroni, as an angel, gave the Plates of Gold to Joseph Smith. With the power of God, Joseph Smith translated them into the present-day Book of Mormon.**

KELLIE: **Shannon, you just mentioned another set of Plates; the Plates of Ether. What are those?** (Shannon look at the others for help)

TRACY: Part of the history of the Jaredites. Moroni did not include the first part. He assumed that, since the Jews already had it, the people of our time would too.

AMBER: Why would the Jews have it?

SHANNON: Because they were the people who built the Tower of Babel.

LAUREL: Well, they were among the people who lived in Babel at the time the tower was built.

DANIEL: Kellie will you read Genesis 11: 4-9? Then Autumn, will you follow with Ether 1:33?

KELLIE: And they said, Go to, let us build us a city and a tower, whose top may reach unto Heaven; and let us make us a name, lest we be scattered abroad upon the face of the whole earth.

And the Lord came down to see the city and the tower, which the children of men builded.

And the Lord said, Behold, the people is one, and they have all one language; and this they begin to do.

Go to, let us go down, and there confound their language, that they may not understand one another's speech.

So, the Lord scattered them abroad from thence upon the face of all the earth: and they left off to build the city.

Therefore, is the name of it called Babel; because the Lord did there confound the language of all the earth: and from thence did the Lord scatter them abroad upon the face of all the earth.

AUTUMN: (curtains open slowly, blue stage lights up; Moroni, onstage, reads last line with Autumn) **Jared came forth with his brother and their families, with some**

others and their families, from the great tower, at the time the Lord confounded the language of the people, and swore in His wrath that they should be scattered upon all the face of the earth; and according to the word of the Lord the people were scattered. (spotlight down, P)

SCENE TWENTY
THE STORY OF THE JAREDITES

SCENE: A large boulder is DR, a BPDIA is U and slightly L of the boulder; BPDIA are URC and C; a boulder is L with a BPDIA D and slightly L from it; a table is DL with a stool behind it; a set of Gold Plates, several loose plates, an engraving tool, several scrolls, and a candle are on or around the table

NOTE: Dialogue for this scene comes from Ether 1: 34, 36, 37, 38, 39, 40, 42, Ether 2: 1, 4, 6, 7, 14, 16, 18, Ether 3: 2, 3, 4, 6, 9, 10, 11, 12, 13, Ether 5: 1, 4, 11, 12

AT RISE: The Brother of Jared and Jared are standing together L of the boulder DR; Moroni is seated at the stone table, writing; Moroni reads Autumn's last line with her, as the curtain opens, footlight up

MORONI: (read with Autumn) **. . . and according to the word of the Lord the people were scattered**

(read alone) **And the Brother of Jared, being a large and mighty man, and a man highly favored of the Lord, Jared, his brother, said unto him:** (spotlight up, DR)

JARED: **Cry unto the Lord, that He will not confound us that we may not understand our words.**

MORONI: **Then Jared said unto his brother:**

JARED: **Cry again unto the Lord, and it may be that He will turn away His anger from them who are our friends, that He confound not their language.**

85

MORONI: And it came to pass that Jared spake again unto his brother, saying:

JARED: Go and inquire of the Lord whether He will drive us out of the land, and if He will drive us out of the land, cry unto Him whither we shall go. (Jared exits DR)

MORONI: (I FEEL MY SAVIOR'S LOVE begins playing in the background; stage action precedes narration) **And it came to pass that the Brother of Jared did cry unto the Lord according to that which had been spoken by the mouth of Jared. And it came to pass that the Lord did hear the Brother of Jared, and had compassion upon him, and said unto him:**

VOICE OF GOD: Go to and gather together thy flocks, and the seed of the earth of every kind, and thy families, and also Jared, thy brother and his families, and also thy friends and their families, and the friends of Jared and their families. And when thou hast done this thou shalt go at the head of them down into the valley which is northward. And there will I meet thee, and I will go before thee into a land which is choice above all the lands of the earth.

MORONI: (the Brother of Jared exits DR, re-enters with a small group UR; they mill about UR; the Brother of Jared removes himself from the group, moves DR to boulders, kneels facing off stage) **And it came to pass that they went down into the valley (the name of which was Nimrod). And it came to pass that the Lord came down and talked with the Brother of Jared; and He was in a cloud and the Brother of Jared saw Him not. And it came to pass that the Lord commanded them that they should go forth into the wilderness.** (the Brother of Jared rises, returns to the group; group crossed UC, circle BPDIA, spread out over RC, C, and DC) **They traveled into the wilderness and did build barges, in which they**

did cross many waters, being directed continually by the hand of the Lord. (group gradually disperses, exiting R and L; the Brother of Jared remains UL) **And the Lord would not suffer that they should stop beyond the sea in the wilderness, but He would that they should come forth even unto the Land of Promise. And it came to pass, at the end of four years that Lord said:**

VOICE OF GOD: **Go to work and build after the manner of barges, which ye have hitherto built.** (the Brother of Jared kneels at boulder, facing off stage)

MORONI: **And it came to pass that the Brother of Jared and his brethren did build barges. And it came to pass that the Brother of Jared cried unto the Lord:**

BROTHER OF JARED: **O Lord, Thou hast said that we must be encompassed about by the floods. Suffer not that they shall go forth across this raging deep in darkness, but behold these things which I have molten out of the rock. O Lord, Thou hast all power and can do whatsoever Thou wilt for the benefit of man. Therefore, touch these stones,** (lays 16 smooth stones on boulder) **O Lord, with Thy finger, and prepare them that they may shine forth in darkness; and they shall shine forth unto us in the vessels.**

MORONI: **And it came to pass that when the Brother of Jared had said these words, behold the Lord stretched forth His hand and touched the stones one by one with His finger.** (hand appears from behind curtain) **And the veil was taken from off the eyes of the Brother of Jared and he saw the finger of the Lord; and it was as the finger of a man, like unto flesh and blood. And the Brother of Jared fell down before the Lord, for he was stuck with fear. And the Lord said unto him:**

VOICE OF GOD: Because of thy faith, thou hast seen that I shall take upon Me flesh and blood. And never has man come before Me with such exceeding faith as thou hast, for were it not so, ye could not have seen My finger. Sawest thou more than this?

BROTHER OF JARED: Nay, Lord; show Thyself unto me.

VOICE OF GOD: Believest thou the words which I shall speak?

BROTHER OF JARED: Yea, Lord, I know that Thou speakest the truth, for Thou art a God of truth and canst not lie.

MORONI: (Brother of Jared looks up with awe; Jesus is not visible to the audience; a light shines from back stage) **And when he had said these words, behold, the Lord showed Himself unto him. And now I, Moroni, proceed to give the record of Jared and his brother.** (spotlight down; music ends; the Brother of Jared exits UL) **For it came to pass that they got aboard their barges and set forth into the sea and were driven forth, three hundred and forty and four days upon the water. And they did land upon the shore of the Promised Land.** (stage lights and footlights down; curtain closes)

SCENE TWENTY ONE

DANIEL: (spotlight up, P) **The Jaredites lived in the north lands of the Americas. They eventually fell into wickedness and, through war, destroyed themselves. But they left their record behind and it was found by the Nephites.**

RYAN: **That is a remarkable story! All the stories you have told tonight are awesome, but this one is particularly interesting because it's . . . it's like part two of a story that begins in the Bible. I am curious, though; Jesus lived among the Jews, so, they knew firsthand of His reality. Did anyone in Ancient America, any group of people, ever see Jesus in the flesh?**

HEATHER: Oh, yes! Here, (she hands him a Bible) **read John 10:16**

RYAN: **And other sheep I have, which are not of this fold. Them also I must bring and they shall hear My voice, and there shall be one fold and one shepherd.**

TRACY: **Those other sheep were the ancient Americans.**

WAYNE: **The people were looking for the Savior's coming just as the people of Jerusalem had been. Christ's ministry to the Jewish people took place during His mortal state. His ministry to the Nephites happened after His resurrection.**

SHANNON: **The people on the American continent knew of the Savior's birth because there was a new star in the Heavens, after a day and a night and a day of light. The sign of His death and coming to the Americas was three days and nights of darkness.** (spotlight down, P)

SCENE TWENTY TWO
THE COMING OF CHRIST TO THE AMERICAS

SCENE: The auditorium is in total darkness; Multitudes enter auditorium DR, UR, and UL and filter among and around audience; some stand, some sit on the floor, some kneel

NOTE: Dialogue for this scene is taken from 3 Nephi 8: 5, 6, 7, 8, 9, 10, 12, 19, 20, 21, 22, 23, 24, 25; 3 Nephi 9: 2, 13, 14, 15, 16, 18, 20, 22; 3 Nephi 11: 7, 11, 23, 28, 29, 30, 37, 38, 39, 41

DANIEL: **And it came to pass in the thirty and fourth year, in the first month, on the fourth day of the month, there arose a great storm,** (behind curtain, stage lights flash; footlights flash; a sound effects recording of thunder, tremendous winds, crashing waves, sounds of earthquakes, buildings falling, and torrential rains begins to play:

Note: all of these sounds should be individually recorded; they can be played on separate recorders so as to enable the emphasis of individual sounds according to text, or they can be mixed on one tape, with individual sounds being heard over other sounds at appropriate moments as determined by text.

Tension is created by the rapid bow action of a high cord on a violin AND the repetitious striking of two low keys on a piano; the sound effects tape begins relatively low; Daniel's voice must be heard over the noise; volume will gradually increase during the narration) **There was also a great and terrible tempest. There was terrible thunder, insomuch that it did shake the whole earth. There were exceedingly sharp lightnings, and the city Zarahemla did take fire. The city of Moroni did sink into the depth of the sea. The earth was carried up upon the city of**

Moronihah, that in the place of the city, there became a great mountain. The whole face of the land was changed because of the tempest and the whirlwinds and the thunderings and the lightnings and the exceeding great quaking of the whole earth. (the sound mounts to a tremendous level, the vibrations of which give the effect of movement; continue the effects for approximately one minute beyond the narrative; during this time, pieces of buildings and broken columns are thrown onto the auditorium floor, four BPDIA are moved onto the proscenium, DR, DRC, DLC, and DL) **And it came to pass that when the thunderings and the lightnings and, storm and the tempest, and the quaking's of the earth did cease** (all sounds and lights effects end) **for behold, they did last for about the space of three hours – and then behold, there was darkness upon the face of the land. There was thick darkness upon all the face of the land, insomuch that the inhabitants thereof who had not fallen could feel the vapor of darkness. And there could be no light, neither candle, neither torches, neither could there be fire kindled with exceedingly dry wood. There was not any light seen, neither fire, nor glimmer, neither the sun, nor the moon, nor the stars, for so great were the mists of darkness. And it came to pass that it did last for the space of three days, and there was great mourning, and howling, and weeping among all the people continually.**

MULTITUDE: (howling) **O that we had repented before this great and terrible day.**

MULTITUDE: (wailing) **Then would our brethren have been spared.**

MULTITUDE: (crying) **They would not have been burned int that great city Zarahemla.**

MULTITUDE: (mourning) **O that we had repented before this great and terrible day.**

MULTITUDE:	(weeping) **Had not killed and stoned the prophets and cast them out.**
MULTITUDE:	(grieving) **Then would our mothers and our fair daughters and our children have been spared.**
MULTITUDE:	(sobbing) **And not have been buried up in that great city Moronihah.** (weeping and wailing continues in the dark for approximately one minute beyond last Multitude mourner)
JESUS:	(in darkness) **Wo, Wo, Wo unto this people. Wo unto the inhabitants of the whole earth except they shall repent, for the devil laugheth and his angels rejoice, because of the slain of the fair sons and daughters of My people. And it is because of their iniquity and abominations that they are fallen!** **Many great destructions have I caused to come upon this land and upon this people, because of their wickedness and their abominations. O all ye that are spared because ye were more righteous than they, will ye not now return unto Me and repent of your sins and be converted, that I may heal you? Yea, verily I say unto you, if ye will come unto Me, ye shall have eternal life.** **Behold, Mine arm of mercy is extended towards you, and whosoever will come, him will I receive, and blessed are those who come unto Me. Behold, I am Jesus Christ, the Son of God. I created the heavens and the earth, and all things that in them are. I was with the Father from the beginning. I am in the Father, and the Father is in me, and in Me hath the Father glorified His name.** **I came unto My own and My own received Me not. And the scriptures concerning My coming are fulfilled. I am the light and the life of the world. I am Alpha and Omega, the beginning and the end.** **Ye shall offer for a sacrifice unto Me a broken heart and a contrite Spirit. Him will I baptize with fire and with the Holy Ghost. Behold, I**

have come unto the world to bring redemption unto the world, to save the world from sin. Therefore, whoso repenteth and cometh unto Me as a little child, him will I receive, for of such is the kingdom of God. Behold, for such I have laid down My life, and have taken it up again; therefore repent, and come unto Me ye ends of the earth and be saved.

(approximately thirty seconds of silence)

VOICE OF GOD: (curtain opens to reveal C section of the stage, in darkness; Jesus is standing on the top of a tread-mill, UC)

Behold, My Beloved Son, in whom I am well pleased, in whom I have glorified My name. Here ye Him.

(the smallest and brightest whit spotlight possible is raised on the top of the back-drop)

JESUS: (as the spotlight slowly lowers to the face of Jesus, then gradually opens to encompass all of Him) **Behold, I am Jesus Christ, whom the prophets testified shall come into the world.** (tread-mill is turned on, when Jesus is at the bottom of the tread-mill, He steps off, walks to DC; exits to audience) **I am the light and the life of the world, and I have drunk out of that bitter cup which the Father hath given Me,** (walks among the audience) **and have glorified the Father in taking upon Me the sins of the world, in the which I have suffered the will of the Father in all things from the beginning.**

Verily, I say unto you, that whoso repenteth of his sins through your words, and desireth to be baptized in My name, shall ye baptize. There shall be no disputations among you as there have hitherto been. Neither shall there be disputations among you concerning the points of my doctrine, as there have hitherto been. For verily, verily I say unto you, he that hath the spirit of contention is not of Me, but is of the devil, who is the father of contention and he stireth up the hearts of men to contend with anger, one with another. Behold, this is not my

93

doctrine, to stir up the hearts of men with anger, one against another, but this is my doctrine, that such things should be done away. And again, I say unto you, ye must repent and be baptized in My name and become as a little child, or ye can in nowise inherit the Kingdom of God. Verily, verily, I say unto you, that this is My doctrine and whoso buildeth upon this buildeth upon My rock. The gate of Hell shall not prevail against them. Therefore, go forth unto this people, and declare the words which I have spoken, unto the end of the earth.

(spotlight down; exits auditorium DL; approximately one minute of silent darkness.)

SCENE TWENTY THREE

GUEST: (Very dim lamp light comes up, P) Guest rises, offers prayer

After approximately 30 seconds, a medley of the prelude music and the music used throughout the play begins playing softly as dim house light come up. Music continues as audience exits auditorium.

If refreshments are being served, the medley should continue until the last guest has gone.

Full house light should not come up unto the audience begins to leave their seats.

THE END

But only of the Play